YOU, THIS IS ME

A SOLDIER'S MIND UNWRAPPED AND REVEALED

...OVER?

CLINTON BEAUDEL DOOLEY

Ballast Books, LLC
www.ballastbooks.com

ISBN:
Hardcover: 978-1-966786-32-0
Paperback: 978-1-966786-33-7

Printed in the United States of America

Published by Ballast Books
www.ballastbooks.com

For more information, bulk orders, appearances, or speaking requests,
please email: info@ballastbooks.com

CONTENTS

PREFACE

Hi. My name is Clinton Beaudel Dooley (Beau), and today I feel determined. My goal for *You, This Is Me . . . Over?* is to bring awareness and understanding. I hope this book will serve as a resource and improve community support to help veterans who suffer in silence, with the mission of lowering veteran suicide rates, if not one day eliminating them altogether.

God willing, I will do this by taking you through a never-before-attempted inner journey of my most private thoughts and feelings without regard for how it will make me look and/or how it will affect my so-called professional image once published.

On a personal note, I grew up in a family with veterans who didn't talk about their posttraumatic stress disorder (PTSD), depression, or other war-related problems, and I know firsthand it is a subject that is difficult to broach. An explanation of what we have been through is long overdue. We veterans need to relate what we have been through in some way that doesn't require the telling of actual war stories.

Behind the stoic front of every veteran, I have found a warm, caring protector of the very things that make our freedoms so special. It has been rumored that tough guys do not cry or feel pain like normal people or that they do not express themselves because they are too tough for this type of emotional vulnerability. Well, I am here to tell you that these assumptions are not true at all. So, if you think tough guys do not feel, I am about to prove you so very wrong. Sorry, not sorry! But please enjoy anyway. This collection is not necessarily for you, but it can help you better understand things that are just too potent and volatile to put into words on the spot when a veteran is attempting to talk with a loved one, a counselor, a teammate, or someone else. However, I have done my best to hold nothing back, and I hope these words will help others to begin their own inner journeys of self-discovery, as mine has brought a lot of healing along the way. May God grant us the strength to turn in to our pain instead of running from it, numbing it, or suppressing it!

INTRODUCTION

Here's to you, the brave souls who are about to crest the hill of my mental machine-gun nest. In the next few pages, we are going to be looking deep inside what I call my most secret and hidden boxes—my innermost thoughts and feelings, which I had to find, acknowledge, and come to terms with in order to make myself whole again.

Please, as you continue to read through all these boxes, remember that this all came from one man. Not three or more, but one man who found his hidden talent in the last place he would have ever thought to look for it.

Full disclosure: I currently have a high school education. Furthermore, I graduated from my high school's alternative center. I never excelled in writing, I never read a poem, and I was never exposed to any type of psychology or philosophy. For the longest time, I would avoid writing because I couldn't spell with any confidence. I was easily embarrassed because my difficulty with spelling played directly into my false idea that, somehow, I was stupid compared to everyone else, as evidenced by my constant struggle to succeed in academics within a traditional learning environment. Hell, now that I say it out loud, I realize that I've always been a little special. Ha!

At any rate, I'd be willing to bet that most of you reading this collection have within you very similar suppressed boxes of unprocessed traumatic life experiences. They're most likely just there, way down deep within your subconscious, where the true stuff of nightmares lies in wait. It comes out when you scream in your dreams or when you've had too much to drink, at which point another part of you takes the wheel and continues to use your body like a stolen car. I can personally tell you that after years of war, these boxes become stacked to the ceiling within your own secret room. These unlabeled boxes contain the unacknowledged emotions that most of us had to store away because of our bonds of service to our own country. Remember, we did not fight this war alone.

Some of my brothers from Special Forces and other parts of the special operations community whom I have shared a few of these pieces with specifically told me, "Please don't have your editor polish these writings up too much. We like the fact that when we read your words, Beau, we can tell it's just another one of us pouring out his unfiltered heart onto the pages. It is what makes them resonate at a relatable frequency." So, I understand if some of the things I express seem . . . off-putting to the non-combat-baptized people who may decide to give this book a read out of genuine curiosity. However, remember who my target audience is and why it is so hard for most of us to find the words to express what we carry around inside ourselves as we attempt to find our place back in civilized societies across our planet.

This book is titled *You, This Is Me . . . Over?* because it is a broadcast into the unknowable darkness that isolated me from others. Another way to put it—it is almost like picking up a random radio handset after an apocalyptic event has occurred and asking if there is anybody else still out there, and if so, can they hear my vulnerable voice? It is especially reassuring when someone comes back over the net and replies, "I read you loud and clear. How about me . . . OVER?" I am thankful to report many other veterans who have read this book have responded with understanding and encouragement.

All that aside, have fun with what's to follow because it's not all doom and gloom inside all those unlabeled boxes. In this place, you will also discover hidden talents of expression, cherished memories, and rich healing powers that you might just be willing to believe could be yours too after you read through this collection I have poured out for your mental and spiritual reflection.

So, if I can heal from the trauma of war, then trust me, you can too! I'll add to this storyline in the proceeding pages, but for now, please look deep inside yourself by first looking deep inside me. I'm sure you will be quite surprised by just how many of your own emotional journeys are exemplified by my own words. So, without any further ado . . . I broadcast the following transmission to the world . . . *You, This Is Me . . . Over? Can anybody else out there hear me?*

DAY OF RECKONING

I awoke just before sunrise on January 16, 2021, with a pounding head. My vision was blurry, and my eyes were bloodshot. As my eyes began to water, they finally adjusted to a sight my brain couldn't comprehend. There, sitting in front of me, was my company commander, company sergeant major, team leader, team sergeant, and motorcycle club (MC) charter president, along with a good friend from my days in Germany.

These six men were all sitting across from me in a semicircle, and they all wore troubled and concerned expressions. Confused, I assessed the situation. I was fully clothed and apparently on the couch inside our MC's clubhouse.

I was wearing normal motorcycle riding attire complete with my MC leather vest, or a "cut," as we refer to it. I began to sit up, and as I did so, I patted the inside of my cut to confirm I still had my concealed carry pistol on my person, which had just become second nature after so long.

However, my pistol wasn't on me!

Then I realized it must have finally happened.

So, the first thing I asked of these men was, "Who did I kill?"

The only reason I could figure for my entire chain of command (leadership) and charter president being there was to negotiate my peaceful surrender. I imagined there were dozens of police officers outside. The police wouldn't come in and snatch up a Green Beret (GB) who was wanted for murder and still armed, so I reckoned that these other GBs, whom I have the utmost respect for, must be here to help the police officers take me safely into custody without further loss of life.

To my absolute surprise, someone said, "Beau, you haven't killed anybody yet. But where is your headspace and timing situated at right now, brother?"

"Headspace and timing" is a reference to operating an M2 .50-caliber machine gun. It's a mechanical check we operators do to ensure the weapon is safe to operate/fire. If either of these two mechanical functions is outside the tolerances, even in the slightest, it can cause the weapons system to fail to operate properly or to malfunction and can even cause catastrophic injury to both those who are operating the M2 and anyone within close proximity to the weapon when it's being fired.

It's something we have all done thousands of times as soldiers. I needed no further explanation. I knew what they meant.

I said nothing at first, so one of the men there informed me that my wife had come home from work and found me in a dark corner of our house with a gun to my head. Obviously scared, she had called this individual's wife to get her husband to help her, my wife, get the gun out of my hand. He'd then sent up the red star cluster to my leadership, and it was for this reason that they were all there rallying around me.

As I tried to comprehend the sudden shift in perceived circumstances and professionally answer their collective inquiries, I must have blown a fuse. I felt something inside me just snap, and I immediately broke down into tears, which was no doubt a huge shock for all these men to see because GBs don't do that. We always report, "Good to go!" So, this should give you a good idea of why expressing these uncontrolled emotions went against everything

I believed, as I had to uphold my exterior persona. The thing is that most Special Operations Forces (SOF) operators like me have this hard-as-nails, grind-it-out, we-love-the-suck, and embrace-the-suck kind of exterior because we have learned to be very comfortable being, well, absolutely miserable.

The moment you put that piece of green headgear on your handsome-faced dome, you are declaring to the entire world that you're the kind of player who, when the game is on the line, screams, "I want the fuckin' ball, and I'll punch it in for the team, for the game, for the glory!" But at that moment, I was completely outside that GB persona. I was sobbing in tears in front of other grown-ass warriors. My day of reckoning was finally at hand.

Now, I was finally showing everyone in that room where I had really been for almost an entire year. I imagined it was hard to watch another grown-ass man cry, especially when he was of the warrior breed. I think at some point during the past almost two decades, I hit my emotional, mental, and spiritual wall. I was a man who could take no more—no, not even one more step. But I did what so many other warriors had done. When I was no longer strong enough to keep going, I made our piece of green headgear my identity.

Think about it: A GB, commonly referred to within *You, This Is Me . . . Over?* as piece of green headgear, doesn't have to grieve; a GB doesn't have to fear; and a GB doesn't have to feel or say sorry to anyone because a GB is just an inanimate object, a symbol, a legacy and, when used in the most dangerous ways, a powerful mask. Hiding behind this mask was literally killing me at this point in time. Simply put, I didn't know who I was anymore because, for nearly the past decade, I believed I was a piece of green headgear.

Masks are a byproduct of the Special Forces profession. As a Special Forces operator, you have to be able to control your emotions, your responses, your demeanor, your appearance, your morals, your loyalties, your religious beliefs, and your very humanity, all in an attempt to be the ultimate chameleon, the ultimate operator, the ultimate weapon. So, you work things so that you are one way with your family, another way with your teammates, another way with your leaders, another way with your partner forces, another way with your neighbors, yet another way with your friends, and so on.

Fortunately, all these men sitting across from me were senior seasoned soldiers. All of them no doubt had seen one or more of their brothers-in-arms break down like this before. After many deployments, every person has a breaking point. And sometimes it's not about the number of deployments but about the kinetic environments—and it takes only the one. People who keep deploying year after year to these austere environments run the risk of becoming what I refer to as institutionalized.

Once the operator begins to identify more with the *role* he or she is playing while deployed in combat downrange, the more likely he or she is to reach what I call the tipping point. The tipping point is when the place where you're deployed begins to feel like home, and home is the place where you feel most out of place. If you have served, then you are most likely nodding your head as you read these words, are you not? If you have not served in this capacity and/or been deployed over and over again, then this tipping point may seem like a very strange and backward concept to you, and you may have trouble wrapping your mind around it, but trust me, it's a very real feeling of disconnect. My point is that people who physically make it home may not return mentally, spiritually, or emotionally at the same time as their bodies are being embraced by their loved ones' arms.

So, again, there I was, crying in front of my entire leadership, absolutely beside myself in tears. These men realized I was too far gone to attempt to bring them all up to speed on my headspace and timing, so they quickly adapted and simplified the questions they wanted answers to. The guys asked me to tell them what I needed and then said they would make it happen. I told them with tears running down my face that I needed to go someplace where I could attempt to find myself again. They nodded reassuringly in agreement, and then they did exactly what I'd asked.

My dear friend and former teammate, then the team sergeant, with our team leader took me to the emergency department located on Eglin Air Force Base. There, they made arrangements for me to be admitted into the Military Resilience Unit (MRU) at Emerald Coast Behavioral Health Hospital (ECBH) in Panama City, Florida. There I was, in inpatient, receiving constant treatment for roughly thirty days. I can't say enough about the doctors, the counselors, the staff, and my fellow patients. The truth is that you meet some of the best people at rock bottom.

My team sergeant walked me into the reception area at the mental health hospital. He sat with me and kept me in good spirits while I filled out the basic in-processing paperwork, and he gave me a huge hug just before I walked through the security doors, which would lead me into the secure wing with different mental health wards located within the hospital's interior. I was understandably very nervous walking into the hospital, but as soon as I went through the security doors, I felt this instant and profound release! So much so that the woman taking me through the in-processing observed that I looked amazingly calm to her, although most people are still experiencing the worst day of their lives as they walk through those doors.

I said to her, "Actually, I haven't felt this relieved in I can't tell you how long—relieved because I can be broken, messed-up Beau here. You have no idea how amazing that feels to someone who has pretended for so long to be completely superhuman, good to go, and mission ready!"

I felt almost weightless after all the masks started falling off. All my masks but one, which was so attached to my identity that I dared not disclose it to any member of the staff or any of my fellow patients. I'm referring to my alcoholic mask, which had been a part of my identity since I was in the sixth grade. However, this mask too would fall off about thirty days after I left the ECBH. I talk about this experience in much greater detail in the short story titled "Alcohol Pulls Me In" later on in *You, This Is Me . . . Over?*

Three days before being discharged from ECBH, I asked my doc if I could be granted special access to my cell phone to send my company command a signed form that was time sensitive. He told me it wouldn't be a problem, and at the predetermined time, I was handed my phone. I was amazed at all the missed calls, group chat messages, and texts that had accumulated in just a four-week period. There were hundreds and hundreds! I sent my company the document they needed, and just before turning my phone back in to the nurse who had gotten it out of the control safe for me, I noticed a recent voicemail from one of my very best friends and former teammates, B.B. I listened to it real quick. This is what he said:

> "Beau, I don't know where you are in the world right now, brother, but trust me, I've tried to get a hold of you several times. No one seems to know where you are at. I certainly didn't want to tell you this news through a voicemail, but E.B. is dead. They found his body this past Monday after he failed to report to work. Brother, E.B. killed himself. That's all I can tell you right now. Call me as soon as you get this. And again, I'm so sorry that you're having to learn about E.B.'s suicide via this voicemail. Call me. I love you, brother."

You can imagine how this news hit me, how I felt, and how difficult it was for me to call B.B. back and inform him that the reason I hadn't responded to any of his calls, texts, or other electronic messages was that I was in a mental health hospital under twenty-four-hour suicide watch because just twenty-eight days prior to E.B.'s suicide, I myself had attempted the exact same thing. And I had planned to use the exact same method of departure.

After I got off the phone with B.B., another brother of mine, T.R. from Operational Detachment Alpha (ODA) 0113 (Lucky 13), called me because B.B. had most likely messaged him while he had me on the phone. Talking with T.R. was just as hard as talking with B.B. I felt this huge sense of having let my brothers down, but the real reason I was spiraling was because I was wondering what would have happened if I had sent E.B. some of my writings. What if he could have read "Prisoner of War"? Had he learned he was not alone, would that have changed anything? The reality was that I'd never get a chance to know. So, I walked back inside the MRU, and upon returning my phone, I informed my doc of the news I had just learned. He was obviously concerned for me and worried that this news might cause me to relapse and potentially undermine all the positive strides we had made as a team over the past few weeks. He was absolutely right to think this way, but this time, I did something different from all the other times in my life when I had lost a brother-in-arms.

Unfortunately, in war, you have many moments when you learn about someone getting killed or badly hurt in combat, in training, from a bike wreck, or just when attempting to cross the fucking street. I can honestly tell you that I've never shown much emotion about such things. I would acknowledge the tragedy, but I had developed such a callousness to such things that I couldn't feel anything other than rage, wanting payback for one of our fallen, or resentment toward God, me thinking that his system was complete and utter bullshit.

I only ever allowed myself to say something like, "Damn, that's horrible, but those things happen. What's done is done. Let's go kill them all. Or let me know if I can be of any service to the family."

However, this time, right as I was pushing the pain and the sadness down like I had done countless times before, I stopped and said to myself, *No! This is how I got to this place!* So, I walked into my hospital room, pulled the door almost closed, and fell to a knee, bawling uncontrollably. I mean, I let it out! This time, I grieved right then and there for my brother E.B., and it felt absolutely horrible. However, after I let everything out, screaming, I was able to begin the healing process a couple of days later. Unlike other times, I didn't feel that I had to choke back all the tears with the emotions again upon hearing the news and when I thought about the fact that my brother was dead or when I heard other people talking about E.B.'s tragic situation. Again, I was able to feel it but without being completely overwhelmed by it, which I had experienced before long ago.

SUPPRESSED GRIEF

Grief is a very powerful emotion, and if you hold it in, it eventually comes out one way or another. Take my dad, for example. I adored my father, but when I was only eleven years old, he left my mother and us kids for another woman who had two kids of her own. This crushed me and rocked my entire world! My dad was everything to me, and I needed him very much as I was growing into my body and becoming a young man. A few years later, our strained relationship finally snapped when Dad and I had a catastrophic falling-out. I was only sixteen years old, and for the next several years, we didn't have much of anything resembling a real father-son relationship. After graduating high school in May of 2001, I, as many others did, heard my generation's call to arms after the terrorist attacks of 9/11.

Dad and I found friction in our relationship on the day I called him on September 13, 2001, and told him I was joining the marines to "go kill every last one of those sons of bitches who are responsible for this attack on America and our complete way of life!"

My father was a Vietnam vet, and upon hearing that I was joining up to go fight, he simply asked me where I currently was. I told him where the recruitment offices were located, and he responded with, "That's twenty minutes from where I'm at. I'll be there in ten. And don't you sign a goddamn thing!"

Somehow, Dad was there in less than ten minutes, and I was still standing in line with all the other guys ready to go get some payback. Dad got out of his car and began walking toward me—the walk of a man on fire.

I thought, *Oh shit! He's going to kick my ass right here in front of the freakin' recruiter's office.*

But right before he got to me, he took a huge deep breath. The muscles in his face relaxed, and it was apparent he knew just how important his next few words and actions would be in terms of the overall situation. He simply put his arm around me and asked me to go for a walk with him.

We walked around the shopping center, away from all the recruitment offices. Dad told me that he truly understood my anger and that if he were a younger man, he would be standing in line with me. He said, "Beau, I'm not saying that I don't support you joining the military." On the contrary, he thought the military would be a great fit for me, and he was proud of me for being the kind of young man who would join the military to protect our country. Then, he simply explained the facts at hand.

Fact 1: I wasn't going to be able to get instant gratification. He told me the conventional forces probably wouldn't be able to respond for about a year and that the thoroughbred ponies the United States keeps in the stables for just these kinds of moments were most likely already being spun up and, in a more specialized capacity, already responding to the threat as we spoke, leading him to . . .

Fact 2: I couldn't go with these elite warriors because it was a long road to join their select ranks. He added that I had time to do some homework before joining any branch of the US military.

Fact 3: Joining the military as a knee-jerk reaction was not a good idea because this one decision potentially would make a huge impact on who I'd be, where I'd be, and what I'd do for the rest of my life. He simply didn't want me to make an emotional decision in place of an educated one. And then he did something that he had never, ever done before to me or to anybody else while in front of me! He asked me to do him a favor and promise him that I'd take the necessary time and look at all the branches before joining the military. Despite our falling-out and having been estranged for so many years, my dad was my compass, no doubt a huge reason I felt so lost without him. And I always wanted to make him proud. I joined the army in 2002, and right out of basic training and advanced individual training (AIT), I was sent to Kuwait via Fort Sill, Oklahoma, for what would soon become the Iraq invasion of 2003. After I returned from Iraq in early 2004, my dad and I were what I had always dreamed we would become: best friends. I had my father back for that summer of 2004. Unfortunately, in late September that same year, I called him to see how he was doing, and he made mention that he wasn't feeling great.

After hearing that news, I immediately hauled ass across town to lay eyes on my old man. The last time he had said he wasn't feeling great, we'd gotten him to the hospital minutes before his appendix burst.

I knocked on his door loudly, and when he opened it, he looked like absolute dog shit! So, I told him to jump in my old Ford Bronco, saying I was taking him to the hospital one way or another. I wasn't asking; I was telling him. He agreed to go. A few hours later, after he was admitted to the hospital and had completed a bunch of initial tests and imaging, I was sitting in the room with him when his doctor finally came in with the news.

"Mr. Dooley, I regret having to inform you of this, but you have cancer. It's pretty far along, and there is a lot of it. So, we need to begin aggressive treatments immediately."

I looked at Dad in utter shock. Dad just sat back, told the doctor that he understood, and asked him to please do whatever he could. Six weeks later, Dad died at fifty-four years old while I held his hand and felt his heart beat for the very last time.

Dad, like so many other veterans in Vietnam, had been exposed to Agent Orange, and like so many other Vietnam vets, he never asked the Office of Veterans Affairs (VA) for a single thing. Hell, he wasn't even enrolled with the VA to my knowledge. His logic was something like, "I don't want to take a seat away from those who really need the help." My dad was selfless to a fault.

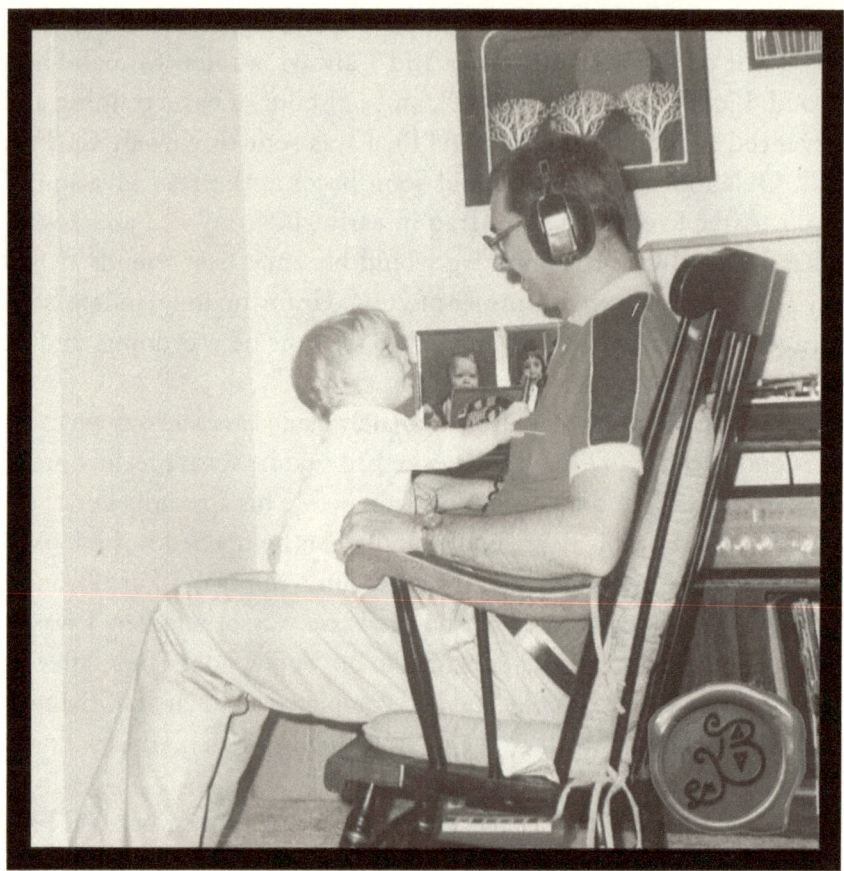

Initially, I had joined the Oklahoma Army Reserves in the hopes of not only serving our country but also earning a chance to get a college education. However, after Dad died, all I wanted to do was go join him, and I knew just the place to achieve that end.

So, I dropped out of my first year of community college and signed three-year papers for active duty. I asked for the Eighty-Second Airborne Division, but I had to go with the needs of the army. Thus, I was given a different noncombat arms military occupational specialty (MOS)—a job. A few years later, I was approached by some GBs—J.H., M.B., and R.S.—who had played rugby with me as part of the Fort Bragg Rugby Club in 2007.

"Miss you, mates! Now go shoot the boot!"

They had heard I felt unfulfilled working with the conventional side of the military, and they challenged me to go to Special Forces Assessment and Selection (SFAS). Let's put it this way: I went from just having a drink after a Thursday practice with these guys to meeting them at 0500 the following Monday to do a physical fitness test, and this led to me starting SFAS the following Monday. So, ten days later, having spent most of my time in selection, I was wondering what the hell a GB even was, but I eventually got the gist of it. Simply put, GB is learning to be comfortable with being really, really uncomfortable!

After the qualification course, which was a little longer than a year at that time in 2008–2009, I pulled some strings after getting assigned to Tenth Special Forces Group Airborne at Fort Carson located in Colorado. I wanted First Battalion, Tenth Special Forces Group (SFG) Airborne, located in Stuttgart, Germany, because that unit had just landed itself back into the combat deployment lineup for Afghanistan. If I had gone to Tenth Main at that time, I would have most likely only deployed to places like Africa, which is no walk in the park, but it just wasn't what I was longing for. I was salivating for a piece of the fight in Afghanistan!

Side note: On the day I graduated from the John F. Kennedy Special Warfare Center and School as a brand-new GB 18B (weapons sergeant), J.H., who had talked to me about going to SFAS, asked me to go for a ride with him over to the Special Forces Association (SFA) in Fayetteville, North Carolina. He could still see just how eager I was to fight. He said something profound, but at that time, I couldn't hear the wisdom contained within his words. But, boy, I sure do understand them now. And I'm quite sure some of my readers understand them very well too.

J.H. said, "Beau, everybody is eager for a fight until they get humbled, and afterward, there is never quite the same lust for it again. Also, brother, be careful what you go looking for because it just might be out there looking for you too!"

J.H. (the Silver Fox) is very, very wise!

After multiple combat deployments to Afghanistan, I left active duty in October 2012. My wife, Emmy—you will soon learn just how important she has been in my life—whom I met on July 4, 2005, and I had been geographically separated since our relationship's inception, which at the time had already been on for seven long years! My wife's mother had tragically died in a car accident in early January 2011. I went home to be with my Emmy when we laid her mother to rest, but I would not be able to join her for another eighteen months, the reason being that I was serving on Special Forces Operational Detachment Alpha (SFODA) Team 0113, otherwise referred to as Lucky 13, and as I mentioned previously, our ODA was ordered to do back-to-back deployments to Afghanistan. Emmy especially knew I would never let my mates go back to Afghanistan without me. I would explain to Emmy during marriage counseling years later that this one decision absolutely fractured me deep inside.

You see, before my mother-in-law's tragic death, I knew my Emmy had all the support she would ever need, whether I came back busted up and alive or came back a true hero in a casket. Emmy would be just fine in the end. This reassurance allowed me to solely focus on my mission. However, after her mother's untimely death, I knew she needed me in the worst of ways. I had sworn to protect her no matter what, and I was also honor-bound to put her second for the good of the mission and my team. So, my heart stayed right there with her in Oklahoma, but my ass went right back to war in order to stand shoulder to shoulder with my brothers from Lucky 13. That next deployment, the guys could tell something wasn't quite right with me in the head and heart. It's now very clear it was because my heart was broken in half and was half a world away.

In late 2012, I had recently arrived back from Germany, and Emmy and I were finally living under the same roof like a conventional married couple. One morning, she came up to me in our kitchen while I was making myself a protein shake. She grabbed my arm tight, asking, "Are you OK, babe?"

I had no idea at that time what she could have been referring to, so I simply smiled, saying something to the effect of, "Please don't mess with me before I have my first cup of coffee." However, her eyes had the look of being dead serious.

"You don't remember anything, do you?" she asked.

I asked Emmy to tell me what she was referring to, and she told me that she had awoken in the middle of the night and seen that I wasn't lying in the bed next to her. After some time, she started looking for me around the house, but I was nowhere to be found. As she went back into our bedroom to get her cell phone to call me, she heard something coming from our bathroom. She then explained that she'd found me curled up in a ball around the base of our toilet, sobbing like a baby!

I had no idea what Emmy was talking about, but I also knew she wouldn't kid around about something like that. I told her I felt fine, adding that I had no idea why I would have been doing something that extreme. A few days later, in my office, I was sitting at my desk, looking at my calendar, and all of a sudden, there it was—the date: November 17. That was the day my dad had died. I had not been back home to Oklahoma on that date since his passing in 2004.

Grief doesn't simply go away. It stays deep inside your subconscious mind until you take the time to consciously acknowledge it. Only then can you bravely begin the road to recovery by processing all the heavy, painful emotions that accompany a loss so great that there are no words to express it, not even for me.

Next up is a piece I wrote for my dog Baxter, but I feel a lot of it is my attempt to express what I was feeling as I watched my dad die a slow and painful death.

TEARS

Lovingly dedicated to my most cherished tribe consisting of my queen, Meredith, and our four-legged angels, Ladybug, Lucky, and Baxter Dooley. May we all live together within these words and be born again in the falling tears of our future life.

I cry for him despite his being a dog.

I cry for him, for I am aware he must soon depart.

I cry for him, but not because he is now passing somewhere over a rainbow way up high. No, I cry for him because this feels like a lullaby's final goodbye. I cry here and now

because all our lives inevitably lead us back to this rainbow bridge.

My teardrops fall because this moment is so very precious. I feel it with each beat of my mortal heart. My teardrops fall as I stare deep into his gentle brown eyes, which now express how much he will miss me. My own eyes reflect the same sentiment. I hold him as hard as I can and for as long as I can against the walls of my breaking heart as he and I breathe together, now and forever,

crying together, here and forever, as we release love's gift back to an eternal truth. Now cry for us as time slips through our fingers like ashes. We who are from ashes become ashes again, ashes covering the fields where the flower now grows.

Tears just keep falling as love leaves its calling within each teardrop. We all cry for love over the years, crying countless tears. Tears are the spaces between each of our lives' ending chapters—

showers of tears scattered over the oceans. Tears will fall for you too, you who now toast and raise your glasses over your own loved ones' ashes—

splashes of tears from cheeks to beers. Tears just keep falling with each sunset. Ashes keep burning as the world keeps on turning.

We cry again, again, and again
as we live again,

as we lose again,
as we love again.

These tears in my beer are for you, you who now cry,

crying in pain as another chapter now begins. In our time, we expressed it the same, with all the pain, teardrops, and ashes mixing together, forming the very substance of life and love.

I've since continued to help my wife cope with the grief of losing her mother. It's taken many years for her to finally tune in to her own pain after her mother's sudden death. All you can do for your spouse is be there for them because it's their pain, not yours! Just like your pain is not anybody else's burden to bear. Though it's only human nature to try to find someone to help share the burden, the pain is yours and yours alone as far as the subconscious is concerned. Others can help tremendously, once and only if you help yourself. Sometimes it's a very long and strenuous journey processing your own world-shattering grief, but please believe me that it's possible. I have no reason to speak falsely to you now.

Combat comes with a lot of grief and unprocessed emotions. If PTSD were a credit card, you'd never willingly apply for it because of the ridiculously high interest rate. Veterans are killing themselves every single day because they see no way out from under the burden of this relentlessly persistent compounding mental and spiritual debt. I see a lot of veterans now who are running from the creditors of war. The fortunate ones like me are those who found help after declaring emotional bankruptcy before falling victim to the foreclosure of suicide.

From the earliest age I can remember, I was around combat veterans with PTSD. Both of my grandfathers fought in World War II, and my dad fought in Vietnam. All the Vietnam vets in our small town would regularly come by our house to see Dad when I was a child. They would show up at random times on the weekends when they noticed Dad's truck parked outside. Typically, they were all pretty quiet, and the group always had a thirty-pack of original Coors Banquet beer set out for all the group's enjoyment. And once the first thirty-pack was inevitably gone, they always had another one to replace it. Regularly, after the second thirty-pack was opened, the PTSD and their unprocessed grief would come to the surface. Sometimes, Dad would have to grab one of them up and remind them where they were. One time, my dad just kept telling one of his fellow veterans, "We're not in Vietnam anymore, brother. We are all back home, and everything is OK again. Come back to us. Come on back!"

Other times, they would drink and teach me things. For example, I learned how to cause a human trachea to collapse before I even knew how to throw a football, and that's saying something considering I was born and raised in the football state of Oklahoma!

I also remember being astonished as a child when my dad and grandfather were around each other at the family farmhouse where both my grandparents lived and where my dad and both his siblings had been raised. It was as if these two men were communicating with each other without saying a word. They just seemed to be comforting each other by their very presence in some strange and unexplained way. I now understand this phenomenon all too well.

Veterans need each other because some things you just had to be there to understand. There is an unspoken trust when we know someone else understands what we are also carrying around deep within us, and this fact causes us to relax. I can tell you from firsthand experience—and I already mentioned this earlier, but it's so important that I will restate it here—that while, physically speaking, the United States has brought back most of our veterans, it doesn't mean they have been safely brought back home to their families and their communities or reestablished any of their lost faith in humanity.

Veteran suicide due to PTSD may very well be our generation's "Agent Orange." Our country has *not* done its duty for these men and women, and the duty won't be complete until the total service member is put back together as well as can be or as close to what he or she was upon entering the service to defend our nation. And it doesn't matter what country the individual hails from during a time of global war. Veteran suicide is not only a red, white, and blue issue. We all must strive on behalf of our patriots no matter what flag flies high over our homes!

You, This Is Me . . . Over? is dedicated to those who suffer in silence and to the family members who are trying to understand what their loved one has been through or is still going through. We press forward to help mend and repair as many relationships as possible for the children who were affected by a parent's service, which has resulted in

PTSD and suffering in silence. We also endeavor to give hope to those veterans who are either hospitalized at the moment or sitting at home suffering from the silent killer of mental illness, which is one of the repercussions of combat.

> God grant us the serenity to accept the things we cannot change, the courage to change the things we can, and the wisdom to know the difference. Amen.
>
> —Serenity Prayer

PART I

LOVE LEAVING TO GO TO WAR

LOVE ME NOW

Love me now, in the presence of all.
Love me now, embracing the fall.

Love me now and let go of your pride. Love me now as our two hearts collide. Love me now with the wind off your lips. Love me now as my heart flutters and skips. Love me now with your healing touch, my goddess. Love me now, and please don't be so modest. Love me now while my eyes see only you. Love me now with kisses that are as sweet as honeydew. Love me now with a passion *insane*!

Love me now without desire *restrained*!

Love me now, before it is too late. Love me now, and show me it is fate.

LOVERS, FIGHTERS, QUITTERS

Lovers love, fighters fight, quitters quit—this is the sum of all of it. Two people meet and start their lives, never knowing the struggles behind red eyes. They embrace the nights with gazing eyes, melting holes in each other's hearts. Life is bitter, life is sweet; if you get to the end, you just may earn a treat. But if you die before you awake, meet the Lord—your soul he will take.

We have fought and we have loved and, in certain moments, we have felt above! Cry and shout about all you have loved and lost, the pain remaining. To love is to fight, and to love is to surrender.
To surrender is to love, and to love is to remember.

The quitters, long after leaving, will never feel the love you two have grown in your home together. Nor will they ever feel the pain you now carry in the absence of that love, which is now lost. Lovers love, fighters fight, quitters quit. This is the sum of all of it.

MY QUEEN

*Forever grateful, I am your humble servant
for all eternity, Emmy.*

I need you, want you, dare not live without you. I find peace in your ocean eyes, desire between your precious thighs.

You shake me to my very core, pulling me from my nightmare's door, for all the world presses down upon my mortal shoulders.

The song from your lips lifts the crushing load from my body. Your hands cast the world back into the heavens, where it becomes weightless to the touch.

Your eyes are the stars above, guiding me back to the light as I drift, lost in an endless desert of space and darkness, your arms shielding me from the arrows of disparity, protecting me from hopelessness.

Your mouth pours whispers of sweet honey, potions that ignite a power greater than a thousand suns burning endlessly in my heart for you and you alone. Your hips give birth to the pumping in my heart as our bodies fit together like the final pieces of an unfinished puzzle.

You are my Aphrodite, my goddess, the one true keeper of my heart's key. You have unlocked all that is good in me and have helped chain the dragon deep inside me that only wants to spit fire, hate, and pain upon me and the world around me.

You found me encompassed by a legion of demons. I was lost, outnum-bered, and without the strength to unleash my sword, but with one kiss, you brought a soothing hope to this broken and tormented man.

I was born anew in that moment. You freed my sword from the heavy stone of loneliness, giving me the power to slay my demons and remake my life anew under the power of the rising sun, which brings with it a new day, a new chance, and a love never felt before your kiss.

You are my queen, my love, my life, and my wife for all the ages and eons to come.

On my knees, I gladly place all that is mine and lay it at your feet. I would throw myself upon the very sword you freed if only you were to ask it of me. In this life, there is only your voice, your touch, your kiss. There is only you, my queen!

MY MUSE, MY MUSIC

For my beautiful wife and soulmate, Emmy.

I'll write you the greatest love story ever told. You'll be the prettiest note I'll ever hold. For you are my muse, you are my music. You shake my world. You rattle my soul.

You're the Shakespearean lyrics to my rock and roll. For you are my muse, you are my music. You're not only my journey; you're also my life's destination. You're not solely the *X* on my map; you're also my buried treasure underneath. For you are my muse, you are my music. You're my feathered arrow, the perfect shot. You're my precious pearl within my pirate world. For you are my muse, you are my music. You're my sweet home in Alabama. You're my something wonderful in every night.

For you are my muse, you are my music. You're my somewhere over the rainbow.

You're not just my princess; you're also my bride. For you are my muse, you are my music. You're the romantic in my hopeless comedy. You're my best friend and my long-lost lover. For you are my muse, you are my music. You're the greatest love story ever told.

You're the prettiest note I'll ever hold. For you are my muse, you are my music.

SAIL AWAY WITH ME

I say things that don't make sense anywhere outside my head.
I talk of being alone and being free upon the open seas,

adrift on the free-flowing waters, finding comfort in a harbor's protected waters. Words rattle off my tongue like waves clashing on rocks in frantic tides. Let me be clear: I am a man and nothing more.

Like a bird that needs no cage, a fire burning hot without the rage, I am nothing more than a man with undeniable imperfections. You are like the wind, my love, flowing round my vessel under endless skies. You get worked up and start to spin as I begin my plunge into the great unknown. Are we not the two opposite ends of the same piece of lanyard?

Both connected to the same mechanisms of life without knowing of each other's contributions? Living connected, working in unison, giving each other unknown comfort. Are we not the expressions of each other's efforts, my love?

Tugging and swaying, ever fraying because of the tension of our task at hand. Sail away with me, my opposite. Bring the positive into my negative world. Sail away with me, not to new shores or distant lands.

Be my safe harbor here, and forever, by letting me drop my anchor in your peaceful waters. Sail away with me, free to love, along the tides that I have found in your blue-sky eyes. Sail away with me, my one and only, in this endless ocean of love.

O WARM BED

O warm bed, why do you grip me so only
at the moment of my departure?

As I insert my toes and then my legs, your kiss is as cool as the evening breeze preceding a summer night's storm. As my back pours over you, your supporting fingers are like flat polished stones, rippling as they gently skip across my achy waters. As my head and neck fall upon your pillowed clouds, the weight of this world dissolves into the baseboards of your sturdy foundation. Rejoicing, your heavy arms blanket me, affirming from above the cool comforts of below. You gently push me down the slide of consciousness into a world of my own making. You hold me there as I rock back and forth between the wavy sheets, between the mind and soul. Time flows as a river flows, and moments of our lives fall as a raindrop falls upon the river's current, never to be seen again. Piercing sounds like screeching bells ring, ring, ring in my ears, and I feel a sudden pull as I ascend to the surface of my conscious awareness. A reawakening of my earthly body commences with a single recognition of my obligations, and in this moment, I realize our time has almost come to pass. And in this final moment, this blessed moment, I feel your grip tighten. Your cool kiss has become a warm, soft glow across my entire body, and you beg me not to go. O warm bed, why do you grip me so only at the moment of my departure?

I MUST LEAVE YOU NOW

I kiss you goodbye, not knowing if I'll ever see you again.
You are the only thing that has made my life mean anything.

I kiss you goodbye while our children still sleep. They are the proof we were here and we loved deeply.

I kiss you goodbye. You grab me tight. Your eyes beg me not to go.

I ask God only to bring me home to you or let me die well in the battle to come.

I kiss you goodbye, holding on to the moment until our very last touch. I kiss you goodbye, my love. I am sorry.

HOLD ON

Ripped out of my arms by the cruelest of fates.

Eternity stretches out with the span of each passing second absent of your touch. This, for me, is almost too much. War finds me screaming in unforgettable sorrow. My only purpose here is to reach the morrow. A thousand lives lost whiz by my head. Emotionless faces, no expressions on the dead. Surrounded by mountains, I continue to crawl. Tall, evil mountains, all beginning to fall. No mountains can stop me. I must get back home. Nobody can stop me, not even my own. Daybreak lifts. O 'tis a sight!

We who fought valiantly all through this night—we pick up each other. Together we each strive to fulfill our own promise and come back alive. Time has changed me in this awful place. Reflecting here, I wonder if you'll recognize my face.

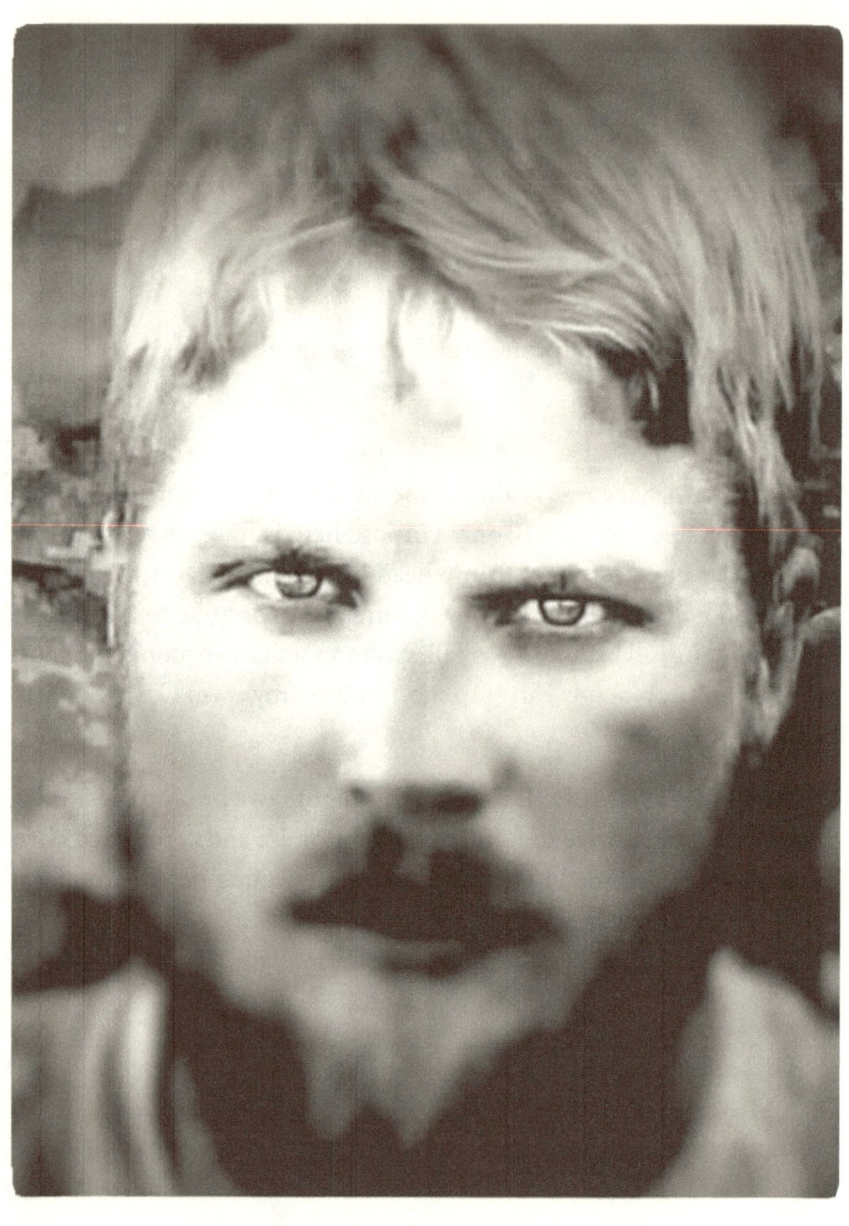

PART II

ECHOES OF TIME

ARLINGTON

Lay me down in the middle of our story.
Lay me down amid our glory.

We live, we breathe, we fight, we die. We love, we leave, we
say goodbye.

In this moment, we close a door and flip the selector on our hearts from
love to war. Desert sands and Hindu walls turn boys to men, who see it
all. Innocence dies inside the soul and leaves behind a lump like coal. But
from the ashes of that which was lost, you find the fields and count the
cost. Dressed right, dressed in columns of stone, we found Arlington.
We call it home. For we have lived and we have died. Now you must go
and you must bide. "Forget us not!" is our cry. We came to fight, and we
were all prepared to die. Lay me down in the middle of our story.

Lay me down amid our glory.

BEAUTIFULLY FORGED WEAPON

Hammers banging,
sparks flying,
fires roaring
as the dead return from their ashes, long
since scattered. Hades's blood begins pooling.
Iron fists are steady, stamping,
dark glassy eyes reflecting amber sparks.
An instrument of death begins to take form
within the flames, Zeus's lightning cracking loud,
Hades's lava pressing heavy, Hephaestus's blacksmith hammer
ringing down,
Ares's sweat perfuming the air as all the gods' labored droplets
rain down from exertion, sizzling on the ageless stones of
Mount Olympus.
Sharp are the edges now formed.

Tightly is man's leather exterior now wrapped.
Aphrodite's sparrows of desire now firmly beat their wings within the
man's blood. Poseidon quickly hardens this beautifully forged weapon
as he plunges it deep into the sea.
A great plume explodes upward from the dark, cold abyss.

This beautifully forged weapon reemerges hardened, tempered, and lethal.

This created man, now compelled by a desire to expand, thirsts for more than Mother Earth can provide.

He envelopes all life within her nature, bringing only death and destruction with each conquest.

With a hanging head, he stands on top of her body's ashes. He finds no rest, no peace, no satisfaction.

Impudently, he gazes up toward the stars within his father's heavens. Brazenly, he points his sword in the direction of his next conquest, desiring more!

SHOULDER TO SHOULDER

Inspired by the film Gettysburg *and in tribute
to the bonds of an eternal brotherhood of war veterans
worthy of remembrance.*

For freedom,
for glory,
for each other—
advance, my brothers!

Loud noises.
Bombs bursting.
Rebel yells heard. Flags flying.
People dying.
Rebels' cries growing only louder. Living here.
Dying there.
Each making peace with his place. For each other we stand
shoulder to shoulder.
Follow your orders.
We fight to the last!

Blood spurts from us
as the hill's soil drinks from us.
Heavy is this day's price.

Some hurt.
Some mourn.
Some dig their own graves.

Here they come again.
Fight, my brothers.
We are all free this day.
We are all here this day.
Fight for each other
as they do.
Fight to the very last!

Cannons bursting
as the hill continues to drink from us.
The carnage reaches a climax
as the dying on each side roll over one another.

Man down,
flag on the ground! Rank or not,
raise it high, Lieutenant!
Shoulder to shoulder, bayonets fixed, we *chaaarrrge*
through the sticks,
down the hill.
Their ranks begin to fold
as the blood spills
on the top of the tiny hill
under God's own sky.
Freedom cries
over this bloodstained hill.
The soil has now become ruby-red mud.
Bloody puddles everywhere begin pouring off the top of this tiny hill.
The sun is almost setting
as the bugle calls us to bed
with much inside each man's head.

The long march home
still seems so far away.
As the old and broken moan,
the dead are laid down inside the ground
But they will not rest.
For they, the dead, march with us still
over every top of every tiny hill to come,
if only in memory.
Shoulder to shoulder,
we who remember
won't let them go.
Our tears have all run dry
because of the dust, the dirt, and our pride.
With this day's work now done, no one dares to say we won.
But we were here this day,
shoulder to shoulder,
fighting and dying for each other,
blood for blood,
bullet for bullet,
brother for brother.
And tomorrow is still to come.
But I wonder
as I gaze across this hallowed ground,
after all this is long passed
and fields again flow green with grass,
will you remember us,
we who fought here together,
shoulder to shoulder?

BLACK CLOUD BATTLEFIELD

Clouds blacker than death itself. Lightning flashes brighter than a thousand flaming arrows, and the sound of thunder roars from the gods of old, racing their immortal horses across the fields of heaven.

A small vessel appears across our bow as it exits this dark, churning battlefield of wind and water.

In the distance, we hear this vessel's captain crying out, "What did we find along the way?"

His men reply, their voices echoing across the water, "We found a storm along the way. It stood between us and the light of day."

Their captain cries out, "What was revealed to us, boys?"

His men reply, "Revealed were our fears, revealed was our pain, revealed was our courage and why we remain."

Their captain cries out, "When all was lost and day was not found, how'd we endure and how'd we not drown?"

His men reply, "Our faith was not in wood or in sail, but in each other, whom we trust enough to follow through hell."

Their captain cries out, "What did you earn, boys?"

His men reply, "We've earned the right to live this day by facing the storm along our way."

Their vessel now passes into the warmth and light of day, and our vessel begins to enter the shadow of the hungry beast of formidable seas and wind.

I, their captain, now feel the piercing cold droplets work their way through the deepest layer of my now drenched clothing. They are drilling into me, into my very foundation, my flesh.

I begin noticing the fear in my men's eyes. They are begging me—nay, pleading with me—to turn from this horrible affliction we must now endure, but I, their captain, will not fail my men in such a way.

So, I muster my courage as best I can, and as our vessel's captain, I cry out, "Men, what have we found along our way?"

My men reply, "We have found a storm along our way. It stands between us and the warmth of day."

As their captain, I cry out, "Now look to your left, now look to your right, and promise each other you're ready to fight!"

My men reply, "We've looked to our left, and we've looked to our right. With God as our witness, we will fight for the light."

A small vessel of unknown origin now disappears in front of our bow, embraced by the gift of daylight and its warmth, as our vessel begins its plunge into the cold abyss, a churning, watery battlefield in Davy Jones's locker.

Zeus continues to stab the sky with his bolts of lightning. Poseidon swirls his hands as ocean waters now bang beneath our vessel's hull, crashing against it as shields clash and bang against an opposing force of heavy cavalry.

Our darkest hour upon us, the men look to me for strength. I, their proud captain, laugh loudly as I look through the storm and I see the day. I see the day!

GLORIOUS DEATH

Glorious death,
bring me home to the place of my father's father. Let me rest from battles old and put down my bloodstained sword, heavy from Caesar's war.

Glorious death,
close these eyes and swiftly cast the boatman across the riverbank. Lend me two pieces of silver and an archer's steady aim to flame the passage of spirit.

Glorious death,
do not shield yourself from me behind Valhalla's gates. Hear me!
I seek you with a warrior's heart that beats with the drums of war and bleeds the Vikings' cry.

Glorious death,
you will not find me in peace and in a kind posture, for I would then not be worthy of your grace. Instead, you will find me where I live, in hate and with fury's temper,
extinguishing our foes with rhythm and laughter.

Glorious death,
let me not be found wanting in my passing moment. Lay me down next to my brothers-in-shield and brothers-in-sword, for I'm ready with blood-soaked attire.

Glorious death,
O glorious of deaths, bring me home and let me rest from battles of old. For I am tired, my sword is heavy, and I am draped in blood-soaked attire, here, praying for you to find me.

VIKING VALLEY — VALHALLA

For a true warrior, E.B. Until Valhalla, my brother.
Until Valhalla.

He awoke by a crashing sea, under an ancient tree.
Roar, splash. Roar, splash. Carved into this tree
was a decorative triple V. Leaves sway, leaves sway.
In disbelief, he stared at this tree as he thought,
Could this really be Viking Valley—Valhalla?

He picked up his sword; he picked up his shield. *Grunt, pull, grunt, pull.*
With sword and shield, he walked through the fields, *rah-row, rah-row.*
He searched all day, looking to fight, because this just had to be Viking
Valley—Valhalla. Not long thereafter, he heard the battle cries: "Rah-
row, rah-row!"

He heard the clash of steel. It was quite a thrill—blood spilled, blood
spilled. With a delighted face, he picked up his pace in what he hoped
was Viking Valley—Valhalla. A fresh bloody fight, his timing just right.
"Hooray! Hooray!" he bellowed loud, plunging into the crowd, *roar,
swing, roar, bang.* His sword soon dripped with blood. They all were
warring in ruby-red mud. This was indeed Viking Valley—Valhalla. At
the end of the fight, he beheld quite a sight (bugle horn, ram horn):
everyone slain arose with a mead in their hands. Cheers, drink. skol,
drink. The fires were burning bright as the feasting went all through the

night in Viking Valley—Valhalla. He may be dead, but he will never be forgotten. Toast, spill, toast, spill.

He found a place. He found his home—hooray, hooray—

Where the brave never die. They simply fight, sing, and come back to life. They do this every day and night in Viking Valley—Valhalla. Now, pick up your swords and shields. Let's go, let's go.

Pick up your swords and shields. Rah-row, rah-row.

Now pick up your sword, then pick up your shield, and everyone go charging into the fields. One day, we all will earn our chance to be among those in Viking Valley—Valhalla.

PART III

VALLEY OF DEATH

THE ARENA TODAY

*For the men in the arena of B/3 Seventh Special
Forces Group Airborne.*

The arena is bigger today than ever before.

No longer does it encircle a single patch of blood-soaked earth at Rome's center. No longer is it limited to only a select few for their viewing pleasure. No longer does the gladiator seek glory in entertainment, weighted against Caesar's prissy thumb. No, my friends, the arena has become much more grand. Now the arena is encircled by the ancient mountains where Alexander the Great himself once stood as a conqueror, where Genghis Khan once led his Mongolian hordes, where empires were formed, and where empires were torn apart.

Today, people of all walks of life are forced to watch, on their televisions, the beautiful savagery as their nation's gladiators yet again push forth into the ancient mountains and valleys where these warriors once again walk through the valley of the shadow of death. These modern-day gladiators display their profession's time-honored craft with overwhelming force and bloody lethality. For today's gladiators, this arena is a second home where they spend not minutes or hours or days killing and dying but rather months and years, carving their legacies into the very fabric of history and writing their names in its blood-inked pages. The arena is much grander today than ever before.

We who are about to die and find glory salute you!

A DEBT OF BLOOD UPON OUR SHOULDERS

A rifle placed into my hands,
Spun and turned upon my shoulder.
A debt of blood now is owed to our
Lady Freedom.
Steady aim with tempered pressure,
Bringing our prey into reach and focus.
We are what men fear most.
We are what goes bump in the night.
Tungsten fangs with emerald eyes,
Sharpened blades with prepped zip ties,
Flash of bang with a puff of smoke
Like flowing water through a choke.
Stitch 'em up, stitch 'em down.
Shot the shoulder—spin 'em round. Hit the pelvis, cork the top.
Did anybody bring a mop? Tag 'em, bag 'em, clear your six. This is how
we get our fix.
Hunting long into the night,
This is where we choose to fight.
Our rifles' suppressors sizzle and smoke.

However, freedom's message rings in our enemies' heads forever, unsuppressed.

The hunters, full from feasting, are never satisfied.

I ask myself, *Does my hand hold this rifle, or does this rifle hold my hand?*

The price of being truly free is a black rifle in patriots' hands, with warriors' shoulders being strong enough to carry our debts for freedom's survival.

BLOOD RUNS DOWNHILL

Blood runs downhill.

We fight and kill each other,
Never learning how to deal with each other.
The dogs of war ravage each other's herds.
Blood runs downhill.
We, the few who kill, grow ill from this carnage.
The taste of blood, once sweet, now has turned bitter.
There is no cure for the impure.
Blood runs downhill.
Burnt flesh and screams do not wash away.
Smoke may clear and blood may drip away from washed hands,
But a dirty soul persists.
Blood runs downhill.

The mirror doesn't lie. It shows what's behind the eyes.
The face may age and the body may break,
But the eyes retain within them the truth:
Blood runs downhill.
We, the damned, scream out in pain.
We seek the rain to wash us clean.
But we have dirtied ourselves in the devil's work.
Blood runs downhill.

THE DRUMS OF WAR

Thump, thump. Thump, thump, thump-thump, bump, bump. Bump-bump, bump-bump.

The drums, the drums, the drums of war.

They beat, they thump, those wicked, wicked drums.

War drums follow me, call to me, torment me in peaceful times.

With each thumping, my grip tightens and pumps,

never letting me put down my sword.

They beat, they thump, these wicked drums of war.

And in an instant, I breathe a sigh, for 'tis a man's fate to fight and die.

Just ask my brothers who share this sigh. Again we must go, and again we must die.

Explosions of battle forced the ringing rattle of a snake inside my head.

Pounding thumps as the rattle screams. I find their true source within my nightmare dreams.

The drums of war are not a distant cry, nor are they made of wood or of stretched hide.

The drums of war were born inside me. The thumps, the bumps: 'twas me. My head plays these drums as I hold

My gun while marching in columns with a war to be won.

The drums, the drums, the drums of war,

They beat, they thump, these wicked drums of war.

Thump, thump. Thump, thump, thump-thump, bump, bump. Bump-bump,
bump-bump.

ROME'S HEART STILL BEATS

Rome's heart still beats

As blood still stirs a savage frenzy inside our souls.

The story of Rome is the story of our own modern-day home.

Warriors are still seeking war, politicians are still seeking power, philosophers are still seeking truth, and citizens

are seeking law and order.

The occultists still hide their alchemies and spiritual sciences in plain sight.

The golden rule that gold rules has never died, has not faded, and has not even dimmed. It lives, it applies, it still

thrives.

There are still social classes among our masses.

Slaves still labor, only now we labor in blue-collared chokers.

Conmen still pose as actual priests of faith, and they still pick the pockets of the poor, though the poor be tattered

and patched.

People brought together from among the masses for violence's sake are still the mob. Some protests are controlled And paid for, as if it were a job.

The Caesars of our world still fear us coming together.

Thus, the few who really rule have learned to stay well out of our public's view.

Through the use of political puppets and propaganda, pulled are our social classes' strings.

They lie to us by choice, depriving us of our united voice. I think our voices did rise together at one time, but we

accepted their gold with all the lies and crime.

Rome did not fall; it merely slipped below the surface.

We together, both the left and the right,

Each row our ships to the cracks of their whips. The whip cracks, and the right side rows in reverse.

The whip cracks again, and the left side rows forward.

Our ship is turned in such ways from the efforts of all of us who now row.

Our vessel has slowly turned to a new direction of their own choosing.

But faster and faster the winds of this new heading push us toward a destination unknown.

We all labor here together, no matter the weather, without knowing where they are truly taking us.

Rome's rule still presses against our very feet, just below each of our respective city's streets.

The drums of war still cry while our soldiers for glory still die.

The crack of the whip, it still burns,

as the world, our Mother, still turns. Rome's heart still beats. Can't you feel Rome's rule just below each and both your feet?

DAY'S END

For our fallen brother J.P., who stood the tallest for us when we were in need of his leadership and strength. BFFB. February 1, 2019.

Here's to today's end with flags raised high across blood-soaked battlefields.

Fires burn, and songs of glory can be heard across the field of battle, over the slain, from the opposing side's encampments.

O to today's end as a thousand stones sharpen a thousand blades in preparation for the morrow and its fight to come.

Men search their courage to shield themselves from sorrow's piercing arrows,

for this day's end has brought with it the passing of a brother whose shield our formation can never replace,

a brave warrior who stood tallest against the rising of our enemy's relentless tide.

The fallen warrior will now forever stand tallest in the memories of those with whom he bled,

those whose eyes looked for him to point the way forward, those whose ears listened for his battle cry to find their untapped strength and courage.

Their hearts will forever feel the chasm created by his shield and the might of his sword, missing from the endless formations, as they march to the drums of war to come.

Here's to today's end with flags raised at half-mast across a blood-stained battle field because a man's flag, which stood the tallest . . . stands no longer.

WHEN THE MUSIC FINALLY STOPS

O Afghanistan,
how did it come to this?
How did we let this happen again?
Why does this cut hurt so deep in my heart?

I came to kill you.
I had much hate in my heart and vengeance in my eyes when we first met all those years ago. I came to kill you all for our fallen towers.
I came ready to kill or be killed by you
like so many conquering soldiers before our time, but something happened to me along the way.
Some of you showed me your faces. Others of you showed me your graces. Some of you showed me your hospitality, while many others of you showed me your loyalty. Some of you fought for us, some of you died for us,
and countless friendships were forged. We were bonded together during our twenty-year march through your ancient lands. Your children's little fingers wrapped tightly around mine as you welcomed us into some of your villages as your honored guests. You even honored me with my tribal name Delawar (one without fear or, simply put, the brave one).

I have heard your calls to prayer rolling across your timeless mountain valleys just moments before first light.

I have seen firsthand the risk that you, our partners, knowingly take in order to come work with us. Each time you leave your homes, you kiss your families goodbye, possibly for the last time, just like we do, never knowing if this is the time you will be captured at a random Taliban checkpoint and executed along the very same roads your families use to travel. To be caught by the Taliban is death. You know this, and I know this.

"But where are you now?" you ask me in your late-night phone calls and messages. "Where are you now?" you ask me with rightful worry and fear in your voices. I owe you the truth, my brothers.

The truth is I used you, we used you, and yes, I know you used us too. *It's just all part of the great game*, we told ourselves. My brothers, do you remember when I asked you how the Taliban could do such horrible things to their own people?

I do, and I remember your answer still to this day. You said to me, my brothers, "TIA. This is Afghanistan. And they, the Taliban, can justify almost anything in the name of holy jihad. It's disgusting, but it's the truth."

You then said to me, "Why do your people not keep and honor your own promises to evacuate us and our families before it is too late?"

With a heavy heart, I say to you now, my brothers, "TIA.

This is America, and they, our political leaders, can justify almost anything in the name of political jihad. It's disgusting, but it's the truth."

I say to you, "I see now that these two seemingly different organizations and cultures are, in the end, not so different after all."

I'm sorry there won't be nearly enough chairs set out for you and your families before the music finally stops. For we both know that when the music finally stops, most of you will be executed in the streets just as soon as the world shifts its attention and cameras away from our shameful betrayal. I am a part of all your deaths, and I have to live with this truth for the remainder of my time here on earth. Forgive me, my brothers. And may God forgive all of us for turning our backs on each other in such ways. Do whatever you have to do, but please listen to me, my brothers, when I tell you: don't be the one left standing at the airport without a chair when

the music finally stops.

WHAT IT'S ALL BEEN FOR

It can't have all been for nothing. Did we fight for nothing?
Did we fight for something?
Do we ever really fight anything more than ourselves?

These are the questions that burn inside my heart on cold, damp days.
We, the fighters on the ground, upon the oceans, or in the air, will
never submit to the idea that it was all for nothing. Because in the end
of each of our journeys, we can see at the very least that we fought for
each other and triumphed, each on our own day. We trained together,
we fought together, we bled together. Neither a president nor any other
politician can ever take away our honor. We who served, and we who
fought, and we who still fight for freedom,
and we who have stared into the eyes of the enemies of our American
way of life have always cried out,
"Not today, al-Qaeda! Not today, Taliban. Not today, ISIS. Just ask the
Soviets, the Vietcong, the Nazis, the Kamikazes, and all the countless
others: not then, and not today!"
Not today, because we own today and each day, and we will stand in
the place we have earned as the most lethal fighting force this planet
has ever known and will ever know. American blood spilled pales in
comparison to the blood we have saved. The blood our enemies spill
will always fall faster and in much larger volumes than the blood of
our honored fallen. We centurions, we gladiators, we patriots from the

home of the brave, will always amass against tyranny, oppression, and slavery. The only thing that can destroy the United States is the United States, something our enemies know better than anyone. Did we fight for nothing?

Who said the fight was even close to being over?

WHAT I LEAVE BEHIND

When I die, what will I leave behind?

Am I a good man? Did I live a noble, humble, or even honorable life? Did I leave the world better than I found it? Or did I attempt to conquer our Mother Earth like so many others who came before me? I don't know.

I would like to think of myself as a good man, but I could just as easily fall victim to my ego's tricks.

The facts are, I believe myself to be a good man, but I live with the heaviness of having dealt some heavy hands. I could attempt to run from my past, but

as I have said to others, then you will only die tired.

Why is it that I can be so accepting, so compassionate, and so loving and, in the very next precious moment of human interaction, be so vengeful?

Life is life, and all life is perfect in its mother's eyes.

I am a consumer, not a creator of life, and our world needs fewer like me.

People regard me, but I'm just attempting to find comfort in my own skin, in my own bed, as I toss and turn, struggling with what's inside my own head.

I look back and see only death.

I look down and see only the dead.

I turn around, and I see only devastation and destruction from my eruption. The simple truth is that when I die, those who knew me here on the surface will cry.

Those who knew the other me, just below the surface, they will rejoice.

Both reactions are just.

I was willing to share my victims' fate, but death has not dealt me that card yet. Most times, I find life to be a crueler lover than death.

All I leave behind is pain.

Everything I hoped to bring into this world has long since been revealed to have been in vain. All in life I hoped to contribute has been left burning in glowing orange-amber fires behind my wrath.

PART IV

FRACTURED

"Abandon all hope ye who enter here."
—Dante's *Inferno*

PRISONER OF WAR

Barred and caged within my mind, a prisoner of my own design.

The guards of guilt.

The warden of war.

My fellow inmates are the disfigured faces of the dead, watching me with empty eyes.

When the lights go out, the voices whisper words of torment in my head.

Shame is my sentence.

My crime is having survived.

For I, a lesser man without children, have lived, while better men's children are held no more.

I dig a tunnel of self-destruction in an effort to escape.

My tools are drugs and alcohol laced with self-pity—

Anything to avoid the now and the guilt I've accumulated.

Deeper and deeper I crawl into a space of isolation.

Those who check on me see only the mask I have left behind.

The voice they hear is nothing more than a forgery of hope, simple prerecorded responses claiming all to be fine.

The truth is, I was never really here because I never really came home.

The man you knew is captured by the past, unable to see a future free from sorrow's heavy chains. Fresh depression

Served daily is my only meal.

All that came before my imprisonment has long since faded from my memory.

Sitting here alone in the dark, I hold in my hands the very key to my jail cell's door.

For I am a prisoner by my own design,

Barred and caged inside my own mind,

Institutionalized by my pain.

Looking for a way out, I pull my key's trigger—

Bang!—

Leaving you all in shock and disbelief.

WALTZING WITH THE DEVIL

The Devil grins while he spins me across the crowd. I see only strangers. This is my life, all full of my strife. There's depression in my regression, with no end in sight. Here, I don't see family. Here, I don't see people—only the costumed masks adorning the masses of sheeple. I am SCREAMING!!!, as if dreaming, choked by my fears, unable to breathe, drowning in tears.

Nails are scratching, thoughts of hurting, a growing pain inside my brain that I cannot explain. The show must go on as the Devil promises me there will be **no more** hurting if I only give in. I give it my all—all I can bear. Trapped in my pain—no one else seems to care. Please, someone HELP ME! **PLEASE!!!** Don't redirect me . . . to another line. I assure you there is NO MORE TIME! Can't you see I'm bleeding?

Here, as I am pleading with my hands raised high up above for just an ounce of your love. Hands over my head, above my insanity, where the voices keep laughing and shouting all around me. They twirl me around . . . again and again. The Devil's orchestra, playing the strings of my stress and the cords of my pain as I inevitably go INSANE! The Devil's bow SCREECHES, tearing across my last bit of sanity, as he continues to play his violent violin inside my head. He gouges music with my sorrows, his fingers never resting, his fingers ALWAYS PRESSING! Pressing into my eyes. Pressing into my soul. Squeezing every little bit of me deep down, down, down . . . into a dark hole. I'm isolated. I'm alone as this horned fiddler plays on. Alone in this crowd, deafeningly loud. Waltzing devils surround me, wearing pretty colored masks over thorny evil faces, spinning and grinning as the music plays on. Please don't forget me . . . please don't resent me . . . I know I'll give in when this song starts again. From the top, he SCREAMS! . . . as the orchestra begins . . . AGAIN.

Baum baum-baum baaaum . . . BAUM. Baum baum-baum baaaum . . . BAUM. WELCOME! My friends, please come and join us. I'll be your new partner, and we can both go WALTZING WITH THE DEVIL . . . Baum baum-baum baaaum . . . BAUM.

NIGHTMARES WIDE AWAKE

It wants me isolated. It wants me alone. It creeps, it crawls, it groans, a succubus, a parasite feasting upon my soul, pushing me down into a dark hole, into isolating loneliness.

Its vines wrap around every bit of my happiness. A weed
within this seed is sprouting. It grows, it roots.
I'm shouting!

It hurts, it aches, it bleeds.

It rips through my life as it feeds. Help me, someone.
Help me, please!

Life's burning down around me. I'm on my knees. I run into the night, all full of darkness. Wicked witches scream words of lawlessness. Owls then hoot. The clock at midnight chimes. Dreams and demons stab my heart countless times. I'm isolated. I'm alone.

I have no place now to call my home. It's been taken from me.

Demons laughing and talking through me: "You're isolated. You're alone. We're wrapped around your very bones."

Shouts and screams.

Nightmares wide awake, not just dreams. They have me; they hate me; they doom me.

> They're here in this little padded room with me. They tauntingly say, "You are isolated. You are alone. This nightmare is now your only home."

MAKE IT RAIN

Pain is the rain that won't stop falling.

I attempt to employ my umbrella with a smile. I desperately reach for my towel of laughter to dry off. Nothing stops this rain.

It just keeps falling, never stalling. It's quite appalling. Can you hear the thunder growling in the distance?

Drip, drop. Pain, stop!

Live, die, want dry, soaked to the bone. Lightning flashes as my razor gashes.

I am the rainmaker. The pain taker no more, I pour myself onto the world that gave me no shelter. May my pain rain upon your stupid cheerful fucking faces and be gone before the thunder in my smile is revealed. There's violence in my silence, a true killer just below the surface.

SOFTLY, SLOWLY

Softly, slowly sway me, choke me, fillet me. Bind me, bite me. Softly, slowly cuff me, hit me. ★ Pervert me, hurt me. Push me, please me. Softly, slowly adore me, explore me. Softly, slowly. Be neither forceful nor hurtful, neither hateful nor ungrateful. Rather, play with me and, perhaps, stay with me. Softly, slowly. Softly, slowly slap me, kiss me. Scratch me, Lust me, cut me. ★ Lick me, taste me. Softly, slowly.

WHAT'S JUST BELOW

You think you like this handsome face? You don't know
what's just below.
You think you'd like to get to know me?
You can't even imagine what's inside me. You think
I'm another nice guy?
Watch me smile and grab you. Gasp! Then you die.
You think you can change me?
Only if you cut up my body into pieces and rearrange me.
You think you are the one to save me?
Your priests won't know my demons' names.
You want me to excite you?
Take your clothes off; watch me bite you.
Take my picture! Are you trying to keep me forever? I want to peel
your skin off and wear you as leather.
You think you know what's just below? You don't know, so please just go.
You think my eyes still hold a soul? Behind the blue, they're as black as coal.
So, you think you like this handsome face? It's time for you to run from
this place.

THE MOON IS UPON ME

The moon is back. With nighttime's glow, I feel a sudden rush from my head to my toes. The beast awakens after midnight's calling. The taste for blood returns to my tongue. Razored teeth overwhelm my smile. Saliva drips then pours from the corners of my mouth. Something in my skin starts to burn. Something in my heart begins to turn. Something in my eyes suddenly goes away as the beast within begins to sway. Ripping off my clothes, this beast sprints into the forest, running, screaming, howling, thirsting, panting, growling, stalking, hunting, and killing everything in his path that is dying. The moon has released what's inside me. In fright, I sprint. Long into the night, I chase this beast, not knowing what I'll do if I find him. I lose myself. Deeper 'n' deeper into this forest, I chase the beast through the darkness with only a little lantern from my inner light. As hard as I run through these trees, I'm never able to catch this beast. I hear the bloody screams. I hear the bloodcurdling cries. I see mutilated bodies with frozen shocked expressions as I'm sprinting by. When morning comes, I'm the one who will have to live with all that this beast has done. O God, please give somebody, anybody, a loaded silver gun. O morning star, way up far, please hurry! For I alone cannot stop this beast. For I alone cannot stop this night. This damn full moon hangs over me, moonlight glowing bright, for the moon is upon me and the beast has been released. The moon is upon me, and this beast will now feast. Someone kill me, please!

BLOOD FOR BLOOD

In a moment, everything good in me goes numb. US KIAs scream across my TV screen.

Red rum has just been poured and boisterously placed before a group of recovering bloodaholics. An agonizing thirst once more tempts my tongue. A deep hate chained within me begins to violently test its jail cell's bricks and mortar. I run to the bathroom and begin splashing cold water on my face, praying that I will not find *him* looking back at me once more in the mirror. I reach for a towel and begin to pat my face dry. I am scared to look up, but I do so anyway, and for just a second, I see myself and think, *Thank you, God!*

But then I see his eyes, the kind of eyes that stare right through a person, and in his eyes, all I see, all I see, are Twin Towers falling!

"Blood for blood" is whispered deep in
my ear, segregating every sympathetic thought of my spirit from my body. Impaired is my humanity when I'm blood-drunk on red rum. O God, will this be the beginning of another twenty-year bender, and if so, what kind of scars and scrapes, and what kind of excruciating hangover, will I wake up with after yet another long night of drunken red rum madness?

HIM TODAY I SAW AGAIN

A man I killed way back when, Him
today I saw again. Today he looked through blue eyes, my own.
His disdain, his pain, his cries, came home. I thought the man I was
back when was thenceforth gone,

but
his laugh I found coming through some unlocked door deep below
the floor of my very core. Deep behind my blue eyes, there is a place
where freedom no longer flies, where all is burning, turning, engulfed
in scorching, screaming, bloodstained earth. Will the fires from inside
begin again to sin and burn the world outside once more?
I killed the man I was back when, so I thought.
But yet again, here we are staring through each other's windows
shades. Which checker box upon my board is his secret door?!

Something not seen from a distance, but persistence is his anger's resis-
tance. Can you kill your former self without the act of dying too?
He grows in my hair. He's more than I can bear. His finger rubs a
creepy smile with jagged teeth through my steamed-up glass shower
door, his face, his grip, beneath my own.
His voice, his screams, come from my own tones. His cold touch. The
hairs on my neck stand up despite the heat of summer. His blood I feel

as it flows rigidly and frigid through my beating heart. Once more
today, through him, I have become what I was
way back when.
Can I kill at last this sick black mass, standing here on top of fragile
glass, made from my own unstable past? Can I kill him without again
falling through and into darkness's chilling void so vast?
A man I killed way back when, Him
today I saw again.

A MAN WORTH KILLING

I've looked for you. Have you looked for me?
A man worth killing.

Is your hair colored sandy? Aren't we a pair of Jim Dandys!
Handsome faces draped over evil, screaming skulls. Not with sticks, but with stones, I want you to break every last one of my bones. Because you understand me, and we only die once this time around. I won't run from you or hide from you. I'll stand here with pride for you. I want you to find me. I want you to see me. Let not another moment slip away from us, please!

I'm smiling. You're wondering.

You're stalking. I'm pondering.
Have you watched me eat at my table?

Have you watched me sleep within my stable? Maybe you have, and have since retracted?
Maybe you're disappointed, now inactive? Wait, don't go!

Perhaps I'm a man you could learn to love to kill?

No, I'm sure I'll surpass all your expectations. Now, stop playing with all my frustrations!

I'm a man who wants to kill you too.

Do you ever just sit there alone in your car,

Watching me from afar in the dark,

Your blood pumping, your heart thumping, your knife sharp?
Yes, my doors are all secured and locked. But how pretty would my body look outlined in chalk?

I wish you good night with each turning out of my lights, one by one by one. Boop!

Knowing you're somewhere out there excites me. O how it frightens me!

Oh, look! I've loaded this gun and chambered some fun. I promise you, my dearest of friends, you will know by the end
that I truly was a man needing to be killed. No cameras, no bars here!
Look, you can see all my cards here!

He-he! with a smile.

You don't like that now, do ya?
My taunting sends a cold shiver right through ya!

You're haunting. I'm laughing. You're gripping. I'm gasping. I wish we could just stay here forever!

Scream for me like I scream for you. Dream of me as I dream of you.
I can feel you surrounding me. I can hear you all around me.

If you're half the killer I am, then come find me.
If you're half the predator I am, then come hunt me.

And if you are half as evil as I am, then God has damned you too!
Will you find me? Will you bind me? Will you dismember me, then grind me?
Remember, we belong to each other. Remember, we belong with each other.

If you test me and best me,

Then please hold me. Console me! Be with me, please, to my last.
Are you there with a gasp? Getting cold with blue skin.

This is it. It's the end! Death really isn't so bad.

Honestly, I'm not even that mad.
What's good for you is good for us. You see, we're apples fallen from the same tree.

Enjoy this beautifully warm pool of blood I've poured out for you. Because either way we slice each other and either way we dice each other, we are each, in the end,
a man worth killing.

FUCKING DEVILS

Drifting into my slumber.

Tearing through my bed frame's lumber. Sweat upon my pillow falls.

Demons hatch inside my skull-way halls, laughing at all my pain-stained walls.

They tap, tap, tap, tap dance through my brain. Raining suicide, these demon bitches. Cuts so deep they all need stitches. Slapping, fucking, biting.

Burning, stabbing, hexing. Pressing, punching, dripping. Lusting, spitting, screaming. One pins me to the floor, asking me, "Do you want some more? He-he-he!"

She's got venom on her tongue, breathing lies into my lungs.

Each breath burns, a hot amber fire fueled by all my heart's desires. The danger of a stranger.

And yes, I tried to tame her.

"A man already damned!" she squeals, her true form now revealed. Pouncing on me, her kill, she rips into my body, shrill.

Feasting on flesh, oh, oh so naughty, wearing parts of me around her neck, oh, oh so gaudy.

But my heart's key is kept far away with my angelic beauty by the bay. My world, my life, my love, my angel, sent from up above. She loves me as I am.

She accepts this bloodstained man.

For she, in truth, is much like me, draped in tainted supple flesh. Am I ever going to win against these demons from within?

The devil's lips keep peck-peck-pecking

at my heart-shaped center-hole lock, but surprise! All you suicide demon bitches, the key is safely stashed away with my angel baby by the bay.

It's deeply in her soul, where you devils cannot go.

We each hide the other's sacred key by the Bluewater Sea, now, always, and forever.

Our impassioned hearts only open together. No devil's weather can even lift in the slightest our love's tethered feathers—no, not one inch.

So, come on, you damn dirty devils, rain upon me, laugh loudly at me, drink of my blood, and peck, peck, peck away. Yes, peck, peck, peck away, you fucking devils.

IMPORTANT TO ME

Oh God, here he comes. Yep, he sees me, and it's about to begin right now.

> "Hey, buddy, how've you been? I've been trying to run into you. It's like you don't want to talk or something, but that can't be so. Ha-ha-ha. Did you see the new episode of—"

The things that are important to me, I rarely talk about.

Instead, I find myself taking refuge inside my head as outwardly I'm having conversation after conversation about things that are frankly just uninteresting, not that thought-provoking, with nothing but mind-numbing subjects that personally I could give two shits about. Yeah, those kinds of things.

These are things I think the group wants to talk about, so in order to be polite, I play along. Sometimes it's a good strategy not to be seen as the wolf among a flock of sheep.

> "Yeah, me and the kids can't get enough of it. It's great. You two should join us sometime."

You know the things I'm internalizing, things that are popular for only a moment, things that other people have only recently heard of. And I can tell they just don't have any real understanding of the information provided. But they can't help but show off how in the know they are, how cool they are, how smart they are, and how up to date on current affairs they are. But nope, not important to me, so I choose my solitude, deep here inside myself. You're welcome to stay until he leaves.

"Hey, which reminds me, did you see what happened in—"

I am too busy watching the weather rolling in and worrying about the storm to follow.

Like a snake, he chooses to conceal his rattle deep inside his own head, the one place he knows no one else can see or hear it.

"You know, I've recently been thinking about investing in a bunch of stocks because of the—"

Inside, I'm screaming as loud as I can, *Can't you hear the drums? Can't you see the dominoes falling like pine trees in the runaway fire's path? Can't you smell the fresh blood on the wind? Can you just please acknowledge what is coming?*

"So that was like our third time in three years getting to go to Walt Dis—"

Like a well-oiled rifle, I rest now, unanimated in the corner, just saving my energy and my singing voice for the concert to come, if only to make a most humble and honest attempt not to be rude.

The truth is that the things that are important to me, I rarely talk about.

NEVER MADE BEAUTIFUL

I have never made anything beautiful.

I'm the guy you know as Clint(on) Beau(del), or just Dooley. It is but an idea. The purpose of this idea has always simply been to attempt to show others how beautiful things really are. And yes, there is beauty in even the scariest and darkest of places.

There is vast beauty in the creators of the day, but also in the creators of the night, both of whom are worthy of being brought into focus for our combined viewing admiration!

Either by birth or by nature,

I relate to beautifully deadly things in all their varying verity and with their endless diversity of form.

I translate beautiful truths into stories or objects that reflect outwardly their sturdy, well-crafted, inward beauty, and yes, sometimes I point out where their deadly outward touchpoints are located.

Honestly, there is something very romantic about being in the presence of another blood-soaked predator, which in my humble opinion is one of the most beautifully interesting and awe-inspiring things in this entire world!

Think about it. Take me as an example—a spiritual being wrapped within flesh and with the blood of a human vessel, otherwise known as a physical body.

All I'm ever attempting to do is survive, survive while trapped in this timeless game of cat and mouse

Against the only real known threat to me in this entire world, which is the people of the masses!

I believe the scariest predators on this planet are the predatory individuals who delegate killing to other predators like me, giving me the ability to go kill on their behalf.

There is something beautifully savage about this act!

Not because these other people aren't killers in their own right, but because, or so I've come to believe, they just don't want to get their souls dirty in the exchange.

Now I am not stating that they are completely unwilling to do the deed themselves, but at the same time, I've come to believe that they are just not comfortable with letting loose the animal that lives within them.

It's true that it becomes harder and harder to put your animalistic nature back into its cage once you've set it free to hunt the only real game worth hunting, which is other human beings.

Now here's the part that really scares me:

Some of these passive killers even have the balls to poke, prod, and/ or intentionally provoke the trained killers, telling us we are somehow wrong for being different, moody, and even dangerous!

I mean, what did you expect?!

Mobs of renegade sparks are falling on or around the powder keg of other nations, other states, and states within states and especially within our own nation at this very moment.

But you can't blame a spark for being a spark, just like you shouldn't blame a shark for being a shark.

If you don't want to be attacked by a shark, then don't jump into the water when there is an obvious feeding frenzy going on just below the surface. If you don't want a powder keg blowing up in your face, then don't play with matches around live ordnance. Simple, right?

All the same, sparks are always falling, all the time falling around us, and in some cases falling directly onto our own containers or, as I like to call them, our "skin shells."

So, just give respect where respect is due and you'll be just fine. But if not,

I'd say we are always just one spark away from mishandling the policy of "live and let live." Freedom is truly a volatile substance once you crack it open, exposing the gunpowder to the spark!

God, there are so many beautifully deadly things to be in awe of in this world, and none of them

I made beautiful. I just see them in a beautifully different way.

ENEMIES

I hate my enemy.

I fight my enemy.

I kill my enemy

in such numbers that I will never be blind again. They fight like us. They die like us.

Your vengeance I have delivered with my sword. I have hated for so long, been in the dark for too long. Lost is my ability to love myself. I find joy in the thrill. I find honor in my kill. The rabbit's hole has no end to it. Many good men have died along the way. I am a man who can no longer speak. For if I compliment those who we fought, then I am the enemy and my loyalty will be questioned. We have fought.

We have died.

We all share scars.

Those not present will never know of the bond between two enemies, enemies who spilled blood for each other's versions of you.

Enemies will continue to exist, but hate no longer has a place within my heart.

MID-INTERSECTION

Hello there again! That got a little intense back there, didn't it? I hope you are enjoying your journey through me thus far because there is a lot more of me to come. Boom phrasing. Ha! But I digress.

No one at the hospital told me to do this, but I felt compelled to write out my self-assigned trauma timeline in order to get a better sense of the things I needed to address with my clinical therapist. So, I grabbed two big sheets of paper and drew two horizontal lines across each one. At first, I just sat there staring at the papers for a few minutes. My first thought, obviously, was to start with my first combat deployment to Iraq in 2003, but after I had labeled each traumatic event in order from that first deployment to what was then the present day, something came to me while I was sitting there at my desk in my room. I noted that throughout the seventeen years of traumatic experiences that made up my military service, the underlying theme was one of me not having done enough.

In a group session a couple of weeks later, I spoke this feeling aloud. My counselor asked me, "Beau, you've done more than most. Why would you ever feel you haven't done enough?"

My reply was something to the effect of, "Because I still have both my arms and legs." So, she responded by asking me the obvious question:

"When will you have done enough, Beau?"

My reply was abrupt and emotional. I said, "When I'm fucking dead!"

After hearing myself speak aloud something so dark and obviously alarming, I went back to my room and sat down with my trauma timeline once more. I knew that there was more to my story than just my military service. I sat there in my room and thought about it for a good while, asking myself questions like, "When was the last time I felt like the boy I remember myself being?" He was happy, amazed, and almost always living in the moment. This line of inquiry led me back to my parents. My dad also had unseen scars, his from Vietnam, which I mentioned earlier. Dad often lost his temper when he drank, but for the most part, he was a happy, joke-telling, hardworking kind of man—that is, until his father passed away suddenly sometime in the early 1990s. After my grandfather George Dooley passed, Dad was never the same guy again. Crown Royal bags began regularly stacking up inside the drawers around our home. Everything came to a head when my parents divorced soon thereafter. I closed the gap between that moment in the fifth grade and my first deployment in 2003, as I had already finished the period from 2003 to then present day. Then I noticed something astounding!

I had written down under that first event the recurring feeling of not being good enough, and then it hit me like a sack of shit: "I'm not good enough" had somehow turned into "I haven't done enough!" I began to realize I'd been running from my past since my parents divorced, which had come as a great and sudden shock to me during my foundational years. I mean, it had happened all those many years ago, and there it still was! I was speechless, but in that moment, with this gained awareness, I knew that somehow I'd just turned a corner in my recovery and that things would get better from this point on.

BIG THREE BREAKTHROUGHS

While a patient of the MRU at ECBH hospital, I had three major breakthroughs that were important enough that I feel compelled to share them with you now. They are as follows:

1. MY PAIN IS NOT SPECIAL

The first breakthrough came when my false illusion that somehow, because my tab stated that I was special, it meant that I had special pain, was shattered. I was surrounded by military members, almost all of whom had no type of combat arms background, and my natural instinct at that time was to assume that I'd be limited in my ability to share with the group for a lack of similar experiences. However, just a couple of days into my stay there, I heard the story of another patient, someone who was much younger than me and who had never seen a day of combat. They bravely shared a story about being a child and having their uncle touch them in gross and inappropriate ways. As this person told their story, I could feel their pain pouring out of them as they attempted to speak about it, and something way deep down inside me was shocked to discover that kind of pain in another person who was not me.

Here it was being carried by another person who, judging from the surface, I just assumed I had nothing in common with, but there it was—my pain! They had it too, and they had gotten it through a whole different set of experiences. But there it was all the same, and I daresay that somehow their pain seemed to surpass my own. However, I learned that it's important during treatment not to maximize and/or minimize your own pain or the pain anybody else expresses. That's when I realized the following:

> Pain is pain, and we are all made equal in pain's presence because it's truly relative to the person experiencing it. This realization crushed my ego, which had lied to me for many years, telling me, *No one can ever help you, Beau, because no one else can ever get you, and no one else has ever felt the hurt or pain that you have been cursed with.*

Absolutely a lie, a malevolent lie, keeping me subservient to my runaway ego!

2. IT'S ALL STILL THERE

The second major realization I had in the hospital was that I had been living my life with a death wish. While receiving therapeutic eye movement desensitization and reprocessing (EMDR) treatment, I was able to unlock many details about my past experiences held in my subconscious, which completely rocked my world because I would have sworn to God Almighty at that time that I had zero recollection of any of them! Simply put, I had not forgotten a damn thing! This was an intense breakthrough in my recovery because I learned then what I hope you can somehow learn now—that everything you think you're free of is still somehow stored within your subconscious. Everything you didn't perhaps have the time, the will, or the maturity to deal with at the moment of each trauma—guess what? It's still there! The trauma exists deep below the surface within us, just screaming to be heard and acknowledged. Cries of abandonment, cries of poverty, cries of guilt, cries of inadequacy, and so forth.

Question: Are you reading *You, This Is Me . . . Over?*, are you reading me, or are you reading yourself right now? Perhaps it could be all of the above? Hmm. Crisscross! But I digress.

3. THE POWER OF THE DISEASED MIND

The third major breakthrough came when my wife was able to send me some of my writings so I could share them with not only my doctors and counselors but also with my fellow patients at the time. The genuine feedback I received from these people is another big reason why I'm sharing them with you now. However, when I got to my poem "Prisoner of War," I fell speechless. You see, while I was redeployed to Afghanistan in 2020, I started to spiral out of control. No one noticed it because I was constantly getting better at my job, like so many of us who are actually the victims of our own success. People usually don't ask too many questions as long as your performance at work doesn't take a sudden nosedive.

One morning, in July of 2020, I came back to my living container and noticed that several of my old friends and fellow GBs on Facebook were doing twenty-two push-ups to create awareness for the twenty-two veterans who committed suicide each and every day.

I felt this huge anger overtake me as I watched them doing their push-ups. I said to myself, *This does not help anybody understand what these veterans are up against! This does not give their families or their doctors any greater insight into the world inside these suffering souls!* I picked up my phone and started typing, my fingers moving quickly as "Prisoner of War" came pouring out of me.

I'd like to make mention that I now realize that if my friends hadn't been doing the things they could do to raise awareness of veteran suicide, I may have never written *You, This Is Me . . . Over?* My point being that if it's stupid and it works, then it's not stupid!

After I set the phone down, I did what I always did: slammed an entire bottle of NyQuil in an attempt to knock myself out for three to five hours, if I was able to sleep at all. I did this day after day, only to get up and do it all over again. When I awoke the following evening before my night shift began, I read for the first time what I had written, and it scared the living shit out of me! The words scared me so much that my ego jumped up and started telling me things like:

*Beau, this isn't how you feel. You are just a creative guy,
and you are channeling what you think they might
be experiencing, but in no way is this you!*

Well, as I read those words again while I sat in a mental health hospital only six months later after attempting to take my own life, I couldn't help but accept them as my truth. "Prisoner of War" was me, and something deep within my subconscious was trying to break through to my conscious self and warn me! However, I refused to listen. Even when I was the one who had written the words, I still couldn't accept them as my own. This is how powerful the diseased ego is, and it almost cost me my life. I wish to God I had accepted those words as my own back in 2020. I will always regret that I didn't get them to my brother E.B. before it was too late for him. So, now that you know more of the backstory of "Prisoner of War," I offer it again next up for your contemplation.

PRISONER OF WAR

Barred and caged within my mind, a prisoner of my own design.

The guards of guilt.

The warden of war.

My fellow inmates are the disfigured faces of the dead, watching me with empty eyes.

When the lights go out, the voices whisper words of torment in my head.

Shame is my sentence.

My crime is having survived.

For I, a lesser man without children, have lived, while better men's children are held no more.

I dig a tunnel of self-destruction in an effort to escape.

My tools are drugs and alcohol laced with self-pity—

Anything to avoid the now and the guilt I've accumulated.

Deeper and deeper I crawl into a space of isolation.

Those who check on me see only the mask I have left behind.

The voice they hear is nothing more than a forgery of hope, simple prerecorded responses claiming all to be fine.

The truth is, I was never really here because I never really came home.

The man you knew is captured by the past, unable to see a future free from sorrow's heavy chains. Fresh depression

Served daily is my only meal.

All that came before my imprisonment has long since faded from
my memory.
Sitting here alone in the dark, I hold in my hands the very key to my
jail cell's door.
For I am a prisoner by my own design,
Barred and caged inside my own mind,
Institutionalized by my pain.
Looking for a way out, I pull my key's trigger—
Bang!—
Leaving you all in shock and disbelief.

HANDSOME-FACED HAND GRENADES

Bottom Line Up Front (BLUF): This is a subject that I hope that you, my reader, will discuss with your mental health care provider.

Hey there, you handsome-faced hand grenades. Yeah, you!

I was looking for a flattering but true way to depict our breed's inherent "handle with care" explosive nature.

After much inward reflection on my own journey, I realized that a man's story can go one of three ways once mental illness takes control, as it did over me.

The first realization was the immeasurable violence I could commit against others. The second was the definitive violence I could commit against my own self. And the third was the immeasurable opportunity for good I could potentially manifest—not only for myself but also for others.

You see, just because I've resecured the pull pin on my mental hand grenade, this doesn't preclude me from realizing just how differently things could have turned out. Example: After you make it through a seriously intense mission, you naturally spend time reflecting on just how fortunate you are to still be alive and just how bad things could have been if even the slightest thing had been altered.

I look at where I am now, and with a heavy heart, I look at how two other brothers' stories ended. From 2020 to 2021 alone, the story of two other HFHGs (handsome-faced hand grenades) whom I knew had outcomes that were drastically different from mine. When I compare their outcomes with mine, I discover a vast spectrum of possibilities.

I pray that I can find a way to bring attention to the tragedy I am attempting to describe in the preceding few paragraphs. But where do I begin?

I am an honorable man, and my other two brothers, whom I will be referring to anonymously out of respect for their families, were both honorable men too. Between the three of us, my analogy will be made concrete because it is based on nothing but documented facts.

Here I present you with three examples of HFHGs:

1. The first HFHG exploded in a crowded suburban area, tragically killing several innocent people.

2. The second HFHG took his own life while he was alone at home, away from anybody else.

3. The third HFHG, being me, was rushed to an inpatient hospital because my wife had found me at home with a gun against my head.

I ask you, which one of these HFHGs is the better man? Take a moment and really think about it.

On first thought, you may say the third HFHG is the better man because I didn't hurt anybody, not even myself, but is this fact really germane to the three outcomes?

Couldn't it also be said that I, the third HFHG, could have just as likely ended up like the second HFHG had my wife not found me that night prior to detonating?

Going a little farther, couldn't it also be proposed that I, the third HFHG, could have just as easily been like the first HFHG—provided I was surrounded by strangers at the time of my detonating?

As I said previously, all three of these men, myself included, at the stage of predetonation or postdetonation were all honorable warriors who had proven themselves time and time again. All three of us had been praised over and over for being prime examples of the best our country could ever hope to produce.

So, why are our three outcomes so drastically different, and why is this happening to us at all? Could it be as terrifyingly simple as chance?

I'm not here to answer these questions for you. What I am here to do is bring my personal insights to this discussion because it's a very real thing that's happening far too often for what I hope is anybody's comfort. The HFHG phenomenon is something no one wants to talk about. Why is it that no one within or outside our close- knit operational communities is able to talk about this phenomenon?

"Why indeed?" you may be asking yourself at this time. Well, allow me to share with you my theory:

It's because we are organizationally run by our egos—huge egos!— which are absolutely required if we are to do what we do to protect the American way of life. A huge ego walks hand in hand with a special type of strong composure and aggressive stance that is needed in our line of work. The different environments where our leaders send us are vast geopolitical areas where our enemies, usually people of a different culture, want to think they are safe. We, your selected warriors, have been chiseled and banged into iron by the blacksmiths of our respective branches, who take pride in each beautifully forged weapon that rolls out of their forges.

The hammer is only a hammer if its metal is harder than the steel that it slams against.

Is this not a truth?

I believe this paradox, this conundrum, is exactly why we, the operational community, are having such a hard time finding a way to discuss such issues within our own ranks. To ask hardened men to open up about their feelings is like asking rock to become lava. It reverses the very conditions in which the rock was formed.

The Global War on Terror (GWOT) asked a generation of soldiers, marines, sailors, and airmen to do something that no other generation before them had ever been asked to do, which was, "Turn it on.

Turn it off. Turn it on. Now turn it off!" over and over again for almost two decades now.

We are honorable, dangerous, explosive warriors who have buried our dead brothers along the blazed trails, all while standing in line with you, the normal everyday person, for a cup of coffee in between our trips to war.

I personally believe our honor is what makes us so susceptible to suicide. We hear the horror stories like that of HFHG no. 1. We all secretly acknowledge that we are just as capable of hurting the very people we have bled to protect as he did. This awareness could lead some of us who are suffering down a very scary road. We could be left with only one honorable action if conditions persist, and one day, we afflicted may realize we can't get the pin reinserted fast enough into our mental hand grenades before we tell ourselves it's too late! We may in fact see ourselves standing around people we love and care for when, all of a sudden, we see our metaphorical grenades hitting the floor absent their pins. So, what would you do? The type of warriors for whom I'm speaking know exactly what they would do: They would jump on their own grenade!

In this context, the suicide of HFHG no. 2 may have been his last-ditch effort to save others from himself. His mind was unquestionably warped and twisted by a mental illness, and this illness possibly made suicide appear to him more like the ultimate act of love, an act of compassion, or one final valorous act of selflessness.

I can't tell you his story, but I can tell you mine because my own inner world was clutched by mental illness that had its roots in my experiences. The high stakes are very real, and suicidal ideation trapped me in a dark, isolated space deep inside myself. I did start thinking along the lines of, *Someone has to prevent those within close proximity to me from being hurt or killed because I'm about to explode!*

What would you do for your family, best friends, and countrymen? All the war veterans who have committed suicide have all had this one thing in common: They *all* proved they were willing to die to protect us.

Hopefully, my thoughts and experiences will lead others through the doors of mental health facilities to begin a dialogue about exactly where the problem stems from in order to prevent what happened to HFHG no. 1 and HFHG no. 2 from happening to soldiers of future generations and their families and communities.

Final thought: When honorable and trusted warrior leaders start performing some of the most unquestionably dishonorable acts a person can think to do, it leads me to wonder, *Maybe, in some cases, the warrior was convinced that what he or she was doing was the most honorable thing that could be done.*

Hopefully this is not just something to think about. I pray it is something that we will begin to talk about.

MAP CHECK

Question   What is the first rule of being lost in the wilderness?

Answer   Admit you are lost, right? I mean, this is not a very
           hard concept to wrap your mind around.

Why are we so resistant to admit we are lost or turned around when navigating through our everyday lives?

I'm pretty sure that anybody who has spent a considerable amount of time in rural environments can admit that at least once during their attempt to break through thick, heavy vegetation, they found themselves turned around or second-guessing their location when looking at the map. Especially after getting chewed up and spat out by a "draw monster," which is what we call the thickest areas of vegetation in low wetlands with swampy areas. Am I wrong?

Don't we all agree that life sometimes has a way of chewing us up at different times? Chewing us up mentally, emotionally, physically, spiritually, or all of the above, only to spit us back out in the exact same place where we started our push through to the other side of life?

I can tell you from my own journeys through some of the harshest terrain that life has to offer that I was completely lost for what seemed like an eternity. Now that I look back on my life's story, the only question that really screams out at me is, *Why didn't I stop sooner?*

Why did I choose ignorance instead of logic? Why did I take the passive stance of "let's see what happens" rather than looking at everything that had already happened? Why did I almost lose everything before I finally admitted to myself or to anybody else that I was so very lost? I was lost for so long that I couldn't even remember what I was even trying to find out there in the vast wilderness of this world. Seriously, not a clue! I was just wandering through life, chasing the adrenaline and danger, hoping that the thing I was unable to remember to look for was somehow going to jump out at me and say, "Here I am! You found me!"

I can see now that me coming so close to falling off the edge of the world came, not from any one major navigational error, but rather from a series of poorly planned and later poorly executed en route decisions. These decisions kept me steadily moving in a direction that would have led any person closer and closer to the edge of despair. So, please take my following experience as an example of what not to do.

I asked myself, "What conditions did I not set for navigating through my life, as no doubt I would have set conditions for any major navigation effort to move overland as I had done for a large number of standard missions or operations?" My answers were as follows:

1. I didn't concretely know what I was attempting to find when I first stepped on the metaphorical trail and began my journey.

2. The first failure inevitably led to the second, in my experience, which was my failure to study the terrain on my map. If I had done that, I would have saved myself from learning a lot of hard lessons once I was in the thick of it.

3. Without understanding the terrain around me, I didn't have a single left- or right-side rail to keep me within a certain corridor, and if I had had a corridor to funnel myself along my journey, I would have had a very easily recognizable backstop as a signal once I had overshot my desired destination.

4. So, with no side rails and no backstop, there were no checkpoints along my path to allow me to confirm that I was moving along my preplanned route.

5. Also, with no checkpoints to be looking for, I was not keeping a respectable pace, which otherwise would have told me just how far I had gone—what distance I had covered—since my last brief stop between movements.

On television, I watched the Twin Towers fall, which compelled me to set out and explore the badlands of war. I stepped into a vast and dangerous wilderness with nothing more than my ego, my anger, and my prime physical prowess at the time to keep me safe from the world's dangers.

Hopefully, you are starting to see just how irresponsible and naive I was and just how lucky I am to have been rescued at all.

Fact: Emotions are not actually places on any physical map.

If you set out on a journey through war expecting to find that piece of you that 9/11 took away, you won't find it. You can't track it down, dig it up, and put that piece of innocence back into your world. Many of us today still bear the scar left from 9/11 on our hearts. We have killed our bodies in exchange for the honor of killing those responsible. I know it feels like we shattered all that was once good inside us by volunteering to take part in this honorable effort, but the good news is that we haven't become that which we set out to stand up against.

There is still plenty that is good and healthy inside each of us. It's way down deep next to our inner spark of the divine. My brothers and sisters, hear me: I know your pain, I know your anger, I know your scars, and I know how dark the world appears when you are filled with the poison of hate and anger. This poison never allows us to see or believe in the beauty within us or the beauty around us in this beautiful world. Here I stand before you to say that I have found love and beauty in this world again—it was waiting for me. You will find these things too when you decide to climb out of the hole you have found yourself in and come back up to the surface of truth. It's here for you too.

Your world is currently covered up by all the thick and heavy emotions that are clogging the low points of your inner terrain. If you don't find the strength to get out of your hole—your draw monster, your depression—then you will die there, just like I almost did.

Question   So, again, what do we do when we realize we are emotionally lost?

Answer   We first need to admit our truth to no one but ourselves, as emotions are not physically locatable places on a map.

I don't care what you have to do or say to yourself to begin your climb back out of your hole—just that you do it, for God's sake, and do it now! Soon thereafter, you'll feel your footing becoming firm again. Once you acknowledge some small amount of progress, you need to continue to move upward emotionally, physically, mentally, and spiritually. Climb, crawl, or even roll if you have no other option, but keep ascending up from your inner terrain.

Once you are out, do not let your ego lead you astray again. You didn't learn any real lessons down in that depression. You simply got yourself out of a hole. You're still just as lost as you were before your fall. Look down, around, and, most importantly, inward at the map of your inner terrain. Can you see the terrain around you? Do you see Heavy Drinking Lake, Can't Sleep Ridge, Nightmare Mountain, Survivor's Guilt Dam, Road Rage Falls, Addicted to Prescription Meds Valley, and so forth? If you do, then you must send up a red star cluster and stay put because people like me are looking for you. We will come to you, but if you keep moving or choose to stay within your draw monster of depression and isolation, then the chances of us ever finding you are almost nil.

I was once where you are now, and now I am home, my home, the place that once seemed like a fool's dream that I dared not to dream. You have a home too and a family who is waiting for you to finally walk through those doors, the same doors that you as a man or a woman likely walked through to leave and go fight. I know it feels like a lifetime ago. You walked out to go serve our country during a global state of war and lost yourself during your journey. It hasn't been a lifetime ago, though. There is still time to live a life that is better than you ever dared dream of, especially now.

If you think no one else could ever love or believe in you again after all you have done, then know that's the mental illness, the diseased mind, the addiction, and the dysfunctional coping mechanisms talking. I was once where you find yourself now, and now I'm home. I'm not asking you to do anything that I haven't already done. Rise anew this day and live free in the knowledge that you have never been alone on this journey! It all had to happen the way it happened in order for you to find this moment of clarity and rise out of your state of being lost to find that you have been made stronger and more capable by the hardships you've faced.

Who knows? One day you could be giving someone else who is lost a heartfelt map check.

REINTEGRATION

After my teammates dropped me off at my truck, which for a month had been parked outside our clubhouse, I returned home to my wife. She and I were both extremely nervous about seeing each other, but we had someone there to help us out. My charter president was at our home when I arrived. I can't thank you enough, C.E., for helping us to reunite in a positive, cordial way.

I sat down and started to tell C.E. and Emmy about all the realizations I'd had while in the hospital. After listening to me talk for a few minutes, Emmy had this look of utter disbelief on her face. I asked her what was wrong, and she asked me if I knew what had really happened the night of January 15. I told her that I couldn't remember much of anything about it, but what I was able to figure out from those who were helping me in the hospital was that I had somehow made an attempt to take my own life. I asked her to tell me what part she thought I was missing. I then learned for the first time what actually happened that night.

After Emmy had found me in the corner with a loaded gun pressed to my temple, she obviously tried to get the gun away from me, but when she came closer, I popped up and pointed the gun at her. She began crying and screaming at me to put it down. At some point, I ejected the round that was in the chamber, caught it, and threw it at her as hard as I could, saying to her, "That one is for you!"

As you can imagine, I was in absolute shock upon hearing this, surprised that no one had explained what actually had happened to me until this moment. I felt almost betrayed. If I had known the full story of what really had transpired that night, I doubt I would have had the courage to come home to her at all.

Emmy continued the story by telling me that she was so scared that she just started screaming at me that she had called the police and they were on the way. I walked out the door. She had no idea where I was going. My wife, however, had not called the police but instead had called the wife (A.E.) of my charter president, who was now sitting next to me while Emmy brought me up to speed on the events of that night.

C.E. then told me everything that happened after he and his wife got the call. They rushed to the house. I was already gone. C.E. then called my team daddy, C.R., and explained the situation. My charter president and team sergeant found me passed out on the couch at our clubhouse. My team daddy then contacted our team leader, D.R., to confirm that they had found me. D.R. then contacted our company commander, J.S., as my team sergeant was contacting our company sergeant major, Ch.R. After this, they all posted up outside the clubhouse, where they stayed all night, making sure I didn't go anywhere. While they were all tense and on guard, C.E. then came into the clubhouse and disarmed me as I was passed out from the booze I'd drunk earlier.

PART V

LAST MASK

"Love takes off masks that we fear we cannot live
without and know we cannot live within."
—James Baldwin

SWIMMING IN MY SKIN

I'm swimming in my skin,
doing laps inside my head.

I walk the plank to my future,
wearing the heavy shackling chains of my past addictions.

Have you ever fallen from the height of grace?
Have you ever ascended through the chaos
in between us and the stars?

If my life's path were displayed on a map, it would be
a figure eight winding back on itself.

Why does it sometimes feel like I've been here before?
Why do the faces of strangers sometimes look familiar to me?

Regard this sticky, tangled spiderweb woven around me. Regard the
glowing electric light from a far-off tavern, beckoning me to my death.

How long can I stay swimming in my skin?

How long can I stay here paddling, doing laps inside my mind?

Remember that last mask I told you about, the one I kept close to my chest even while I was in the hospital? A couple of weeks after I got out of the hospital, my wife and I had a big blowout, and I told her I was going to go live on my little twenty-six-foot sailboat we had, docked about two hundred meters away from our place on the water.

Not long after that, I went for a long day of sailing on a Saturday. It was amazingly peaceful. I loved every minute of it. When I got back to the dock just before sunset, a couple of my neighbors who hadn't seen me for almost a year because I had been in Afghanistan for most of 2020, having noticed I was back, asked me to come have a drink with them over at the Oyster Bar located at the marina just next to my boat slip. I knew I shouldn't drink, but if I were to answer no, I felt they might be forced to ask me why. I was not ready to tell anybody everything that had happened. I choked in that moment and said sure to having a beer with them.

The next morning, I came to on my boat, and I couldn't remember a thing about the night before! I knew it had somehow happened again. I had no idea how bad things were going to be as result of my actions, but I realized that I was an alcoholic, *finally* acknowledging this to myself out loud—crystal clear. The following piece, titled "Alcohol Pulls Me In," is what I began to write that morning after.

ALCOHOL PULLS ME IN

When I drink alcohol, the world moves away from me as I withdraw deeper and deeper into my subconscious until everything fades to black.

I awake the next morning, sometimes in a familiar setting but other times in places I've never been.

The realization that it's happened again washes over me. *What happened? How did I get here?* I search my body for clues that might help me remember. *My hand hurts. That's not good! Did I hurt somebody? Did I fall? Why does this keep happening to me?*

When I was younger, I was self-conscious, afraid that I wouldn't, or even worse *couldn't*, fit into the social structure buzzing around me. I found that drinking helped me come out of my shell, and I found myself freed up to laugh, joke, and carry on conversations with people I'd otherwise be too nervous to approach. But drunk Beau had no fear.

It's been a long time since I had that relationship with alcohol. As I've grown into my body and become more and more comfortable in my own skin, I have learned that I naturally have social gifts. To be completely honest, they were always mine. Alcohol was just a social lubricant that allowed me to bring them out, but now a whole other side of me comes to the surface. Alcohol is truly unique in this one regard. Typically, I find going deeper and deeper into the subconscious enlightens everything, but with alcohol, it was as if the light that makes me, me slips farther and farther away as I sink deeper and deeper into a dark place within myself.

All the pain, hurt, rejection, frustration, grief, and anguish I've felt but have not acknowledged comes screaming to the surface. All the traumas of life, barred and caged below the surface of my consciousness, are still there waiting for their day in court in order to be heard, each emotion desperate to plead its case to a jury of its conscious peers. Why is it so hard for us to hear them out? Why is it that we refuse to call them to the stand in a healthy way, in a constructive setting, and at an appropriate time to review their appeals?

I would later find my jail cell packed with all the unheard emotions screaming louder and louder, "Let us out! You can't keep us locked up in here forever!"

I questioned whether I'd rather hear these emotions out when drunk in the middle of a crowded prison block, where I'd be ripped apart by their rage as they crawled over one another in an effort to be acknowledged, or whether I'd prefer to have my sober conscious bailiff bring them out and calmly put them on the stand in front of a jury of sober, logical adult peers.

Most of these emotions come from childhood traumas that were not dealt with and forced adult-level emotional shocks! Everyone can remember the day when they first learned about death, were forced to choose a parent, and/ or, as was the case for me, were told, "You're the man of the house now. Take care of your siblings and mother."

Really! Isn't that your job, Dad? I need a father. How can I pretend to be that which I am also seeking and in desperate need of?

After working with my mental health counselors to identify, isolate, and bring forth a few of my adolescent emotions, I realized most of them were innocent at the time of their arrest. But my pissed-off child self, not knowing how to process these adult situations, found it necessary to throw these emotions deep down into the middle of his own maximum-security prison, where they have all been caged ever since. Most, if not all, of them have been transformed in some way during the years of their incarceration. Some have turned into fully fledged criminals because of being locked away in these oppressive prison cells I somehow built deep within my own subconscious.

For me, I suppressed a lot of these emotions when I was a child because I wasn't mature enough to know how to properly process them. Now they had become fully institutionalized because of my failure to recognize them. Once I finally began to call these scary thugs to my conscious witness stand, with the help of my counselors, to finally acknowledge them, I saw them shrink in size.

I found a lot of lonely, scared children who looked like former childhood versions of myself taking the stand. All they wanted me to do was to hold them and tell them, "I hear you. I acknowledge you. That did happen to us, and it's not our fault."

I hold my emotional self often now, calling each emotion to the stand. It's heartbreaking to hear their stories and to discover that all they ever wanted was for me to acknowledge their pain, their fears, and their rightful frustrations.

One emotion just missed his dad and wanted to know why he wasn't good enough for his father to stay. This child's emotion was created from rejection, and he began to tell me his story: how I incarcerated him by pushing him deep down into a cell and turning off all the lights, leaving him in absolute darkness, which only added to his already crushing feeling of rejection from our father leaving. He continued to tell me that, throughout my life, he had been screaming for me to answer him! He felt absolutely abandoned once I rejected him too.

He told me how he initially tried coming to me in my dreams as different can't-win scenarios, how he and all the other jailed emotions banded together into prison gang alliances, combining forces to become stronger emotions that could get to the surface of my consciousness. Rejection joined forces with loneliness, and longing became depression. Panic joined forces with frustration, and fear became rage, with these emotions often disguising themselves as extreme competitiveness. Stupidity, poverty, and shame grew into an urge to overcompensate, which deprived me of ever feeling good enough and of ever feeling fulfilled.

We can all learn a lot from our childhood traumas. I know I have. It's ironic and a little poetic to find that which I have always longed for in the world outside myself wasn't out there to be found. It has always been right here inside me.

How could I have expected anything from outside me to understand me and/or comfort me when I did not understand or possess the ability to comfort myself?

Statements like "As above, so below," "Understand in order to be understood," and "The only way out is in" all began to take on a new meaning when I experienced or gained an understanding of what these wise statements were all attempting to lead me to.

PART VI

BROKEN

Opinion: Only when two people are healthy can they really judge where their feelings are and where their relationship is. I knew I loved Emmy more than myself, but I knew we both had to relearn how to communicate, listen, and give each other feedback and do so in a way that wasn't derogatory or passive. But we never had to relearn how to love one another. I used to think love was all a person needed, but I also know it takes two healthy people, a whole lot of love, and patience and fortitude to have a healthy relationship. From reading the following, you will begin to understand just how much I put my wife through and what a queen she has been for loving me through such difficult times.

SHARDS OF GLASS

Shards of my anger are scattered throughout my home. There are fragments of shattered glass across my floors.

No matter how well I clean, these tiny sharp bits of my shame loudly tinkle back at me from across my home's surfaces.

On days when the sun is just right, the light catches these tiny bits of shame, causing me to recall the dishonorable memories of my not-so-distant past.

I was a sickly, grieving man for far too long, and in my anger, I broke many beautiful parcels within our homes, casualties of my rage and its destructive path.

I shattered glasses on the floors, punched holes in our walls, and even decapitated a huge teddy bear that had been a Valentine's Day gift. I also ripped doors off their hinges. On several occasions, I threw wedding rings and, yes, even pointed a gun.

Now patched holes, poor paint jobs, lopsided door hinges, and tiny shards of glass embedded in our carpets represent the battle scars from a war I brought back home with me.

I entered the war to fight. There was a hatred growing inside me. There were the Twin Towers falling inside me. When I opened my doors to enter into a war, the war in kind used this opening to enter back into me. Once I returned home, I thought peace would be my life's prize. However, war then inside me began its countercampaign for my very soul.

Hate is a guerrilla-warfare-style adversary. It survives and thrives on the very things it has set out to overthrow and conquer.

The war had used me and others like me as Trojan horses. The seeds of war within us would lie dormant until we were welcomed home as heroes. And once the ale and spirits began to flow at the victors' celebration, these seeds of war began to sprout, take root, and grow.

With us and through us, the war entered our communities, and many of us, unawares, brought the war into our very homes.

Home, my home, had become the very battlefield that earlier I had sworn to protect, having volunteered to keep the war a safe distance from my home no matter what it cost me.

The world went to war against terror, and a piece of that terror came home inside the many men and women who fought longer than any generation had previously been asked to do to keep it at bay.

Inside our bruised souls, inside our bruised bodies, and inside our bruised brains, there was a pain—a pain that for many of us still pumps through our bruised hearts.

Many of our wives, our families, our friends, our neighbors have come to find themselves on the front lines of a postwar, fighting for their own service member's mental health and for that of the many service members who are still walking or driving around us every single day. These families are desperately attempting to understand their loved ones who suffer in silence.

Our families attempt to free us from the war, but we, the afflicted, often tell ourselves that civilians could never understand what this war really was.

I think now that perhaps they could. And I say in some cases they absolutely do have a basis for understanding!

Our families care for us, do they not? They cry for us. They try to help us put down whatever numbing agent(s) we are abusing in our feeble attempt to push our painful sadness away. We attempt to explain to these people that we are not really drunks or addicts!

But are we not addicted to our own self-pity? And haven't the loving families of those afflicted had the crushing duty, far too often, of mourning us after we do something there is no coming back from?

Like being sentenced to prison or falling victim to the deep-rooted weeds of war by taking our own lives.

Do those who love us not share the misery of war that we have brought home, even when we tried to leave it overseas?

It is a tragic shame. And I did feel ashamed while going through it all. But now I can look back on it with much greater awareness and objectivity.

I realize now that I had been knocked on my ass by the war, and for far too long, I had been too afraid to stand up to my pain, to my shame, to my past, to my childhood, and to my grief.

The seeds of war found a prepared garden bed within me to flourish, and soon my garden became overgrown with the weeds of war that sprouted and took root—namely, mental illness, spiritual illness, and self-destructive behavior.

When my physical body started to fall apart because of overuse, injuries, and the carrying of crushing loads, my confidence went with it. Because of this, over the years, I became resentful of those who still had their physical confidence, whereas I felt trapped within my own flesh.

I was trapped, and no one could help me fight for my own freedom. I had to find the courage within me to fight for myself.

It took me too long to see what my hatred for the enemy really was, and this hatred spread into every part of my existence.

Hate is the dark side of love, which ferments into a very powerful poison. This poison for me was only enhanced by my daily attempts to numb myself with either alcohol or various pharmaceuticals.

These things were like gas poured on a fire, like sticks of dynamite posing as birthday candles—literally depressants to fuel my depression.

The fog of war has since lifted from my life, and the smoke has cleared. My family, my friends, and my amazingly strong wife, Emmy, are still here standing shoulder to shoulder with me.

I look around today, and I see I am encircled, not by my demons, but by an entire army of battle-hardened family members, friends, counselors, leaders, and other recovering veterans.

However, the shards of glass that still twinkle from the corners of my home, and the cracks of my floors continue to remind me of the war I brought through my own front door.

These twinkles are the fragments of the battle I have come through and out of.

But I know many other veterans and their families are currently still exhausting themselves in their almost feeble attempts to pull the weeds of war faster than these weeds can respawn in other areas of the service member's garden, and these families have no idea how, or if, the delicate flowers of their loved ones' past can again find the sunlight long enough to grow through these relentless weeds. Sunshine upon flower petals is but a dream that is something they dare not hold out hope for, for long has this endless fight for the garden been.

May my words be a break in the weeds' canopy, shining bright for those stuck just below their garden's surface, for you still have war's hateful poison coursing through your beating heart.

May my words be a soil treatment and warn those who have not yet been seeded by war.

I and many others like me love you deeply. We are ready to fight for you, now or whenever you are ever in need of our help. But please remember this last piece:

Look for the shards of glass scattered throughout your own life and home. Find the strength to stand up to the one person who is dominating your every experience, who is you.

Stand up to your mind by learning how to silence it, for within your mind is the memory of your past and the creativity to make your future. Both these things are where the seeds of war will plant themselves.

War seeds that take root in the past force you to relive the trauma and pain of combat every single day. This means you are still somehow stuck in the war because you live it every day of your life.

Once the seeds of war have you stuck in your past, they spread and warp your ability to perceive the future. Once this happens, you will see threats around every corner, you will see nothing but the next war that is inevitably to come, and you will close off any possibility of a potentially positive future because with each breath you take, you will be breathing life into that dark future's root system.

If you know you are already there as you read these words, then let me remind you of the real facts at hand. First, your past is in the past, and you can't change your past, so any energy or effort you spend to evade your past is a form of avoidance, which is a form of laziness and shows a lack of openness to new ideas and better possibilities for the future. Second, no one knows the future, but we have survived through our time in combat by being able to perceive every possible outcome all at once, prioritizing the worst-case scenarios so as to be ready for anything and everything that could go wrong.

Think about it. Think about how long we have lived with this mindset of speed, surprise, and violence of action. And since we are still alive, the seeds of war have sprouted into weeds, which we use to keep us in the past and in every worst-case scenario. Therefore, we skip right over the now and go right to predicting all possibilities for the future by steering in the direction of the worst-case scenarios or worst situations from the past.

Are you not beaten down by constantly exercising this vigilance? It's exhausting.

If this is you—and you know these words hold within them a truth for you—then please consider the following:

Possibly you need help. Consider admitting to yourself that neither you nor anybody on this planet is perfect. Consider admitting that you are not the things you have collected (titles, ranks, awards, labels, trophies, bank account balances, etc.). Consider that your physical pain and emotional pain are somehow connected. Consider the fact that you are not alone. The part of you that tells you that you are alone is also a weed of war rooted in your ego, and it tells you this so you won't do the one thing that would cause this weed to die. It tells you that you are alone, that you're weak, and that no one gives two shits about you! No one else has ever or could ever feel your pain because your pain is somehow special (maximizing) or too stupid (minimizing), too trivial, and in comparison to others' pain, not worthy of anyone's help.

The voice of the weeds of war inside my own head was very real to me. It was just as much a part of my daily thought process as anything else. But looking back on it now as I write this, I can see that this false voice always seemed to be whispering deep inside my brain from just behind my ears, and I had to turn inward, not around, to see it for what it really was: a shard of glass, a seed of war, a Trojan horse of terror.

Fact: No one goes to fight a war by themselves. So, why would the war being fought inside you, your home, and your community be any different? We train, we fight, we kill, we die, we mourn, and we recover together.

THE INSANITY OF SUFFERING

The insanity of suffering eventually leads one back to one's own self.

At some point in my journey, I had to be upfront with the man in the mirror who was staring back at me, a man who had made me a slave to his miserable outlook and his aggressive thoughts about everything and everyone around him.

This is how I started to push back at the sad sack of shit staring back at me in the mirror:

> I shouted loudly at him,
>
> "Did you ever truly change the plot of your story's struggles, sir? Did you even change your story's antagonist? Are you truly only now realizing your mistakes? I think your expression of shock is completely false, sir!
>
> "Your story's antagonist is *you*, sir, once again demanding pity for being doomed yet again to suffer the afflictions brought on by your own previous decisions!
>
> "Dare I dig even deeper into my inquiry, sir, and with potential maliciousness on my tongue claim here and now that you were lying.
>
> "When you claimed, 'That's it—I am ready to change!,' you were speaking falsely, sir! False was your exclaimed message then, and false is your message now!

"You did not truly accept your powerlessness over the diseased mind because *you* are my diseased mind!

"And this is the reason why *I* am suffering insanely still. And you will continue to play me a fool, sir, as long as I am able to be made a fool.

"I have been aware of you for some time, sir. You are 100 percent my fault. My fault because I am you. But no more, sir, shall I sit here and suffer you. No more!"

To be aware but to take no action is to suffer!

The insanity of suffering eventually leads one back to one's own self.

PRIDE KILLS

Like a lion, I protect my land, my honor, and, most of all, my pride. My pride is deadly beautiful.
My pride can hunt.
My pride can bite.
My pride can kill.
No one fears my pride more than me.

Before my words leave these pages,
before the noose of time snaps my neck back, let me see your eyes staring back at me from inside your cages I tried to free you from. I tried to love you. I tried to show you that you were never alone.
I desperately tried to hold on to you. I desperately tried to keep my pride away,
but your pride was even stronger than my own. But with my last breath, I will speak these words to warn you still:
After your pride finishes devouring me, it will turn and come for you, for behind all of pride's thrills, pills, sex, and beautifully deadly skills
is a killer. And when a lion, inevitably injured, is no longer able to protect its pride, the pride will turn on the defective lion because
pride kills.

PART VII

RECOVERY

"My grace is sufficient for you, for my power
is made perfect in weakness."
—2 Corinthians 12

SOMETHING ABOUT YOUR MAN

Little lady, let me tell you something about your man.
I met him way back in Afghanistan.
On the outside, he's a strong man, but on the inside,
he's a hurt man.
He's a lion when he holds you tight, but he is also a creature
of the night, needing a pack to go run with
and just have some good fun with.
But God knows we could never, ever take your place.
Yes, hallelujah and amazing grace!
You've got a love that's true.
Your man just wants to hold you long into every cool, dark night.
But when the moon is full and bright, he hears his inner wolf
howl deep inside.
He doesn't want you ever to have to see that side, so he runs
with his pack long into the night.
But he's never, ever far away. With you is where he longs to stay.
But you married that man and loved him all the way
through Afghanistan. He's really trying to come home,
but he needs his space to still go roam.

God, I know he loves you,
but he's trying to find a love for himself too.

He knows it is somewhere deep down inside him,
but his demons still fight him as he dreams into the night.

Trust me when I say, you two are stronger together.
Your man loves you now and forever.

But everything he's currently going through is, in some strange way,
his attempt to find a way back to you.

He still howls at the full moon,

but he prefers roaring by a fire in your living room.
He just needs to find peace

between the tempers of both his beasts. Just give him
this needed time, little lady. He's going to be just fine.

I also had to face demons of my own, and I didn't get
through any of it on my own.

All I can say, little lady, about your man, whom I met way
back in Afghanistan, is

that he's a good man who adores you.
Your love's worth fighting for.

OLD ARMY BUDDY

My old friend, welcome! Dine with me, drink with me.

Let us regale each other and sing of our past conquests.

Let our songs and our laughter ring out as they reverberate across the halls of

Valhalla! A heaviness gently begins to overtake us from the drink of mead.

An old love affair, long since over, has been wakened by our provocative singing.

What was barred has now found an open door.

What was long since pronounced dead is now climbing out of its grave.

O the glory, O the adventure, O the pain. O the anger, O the past, O the disdain.

Our shared experiences are once again pumping inside my veins. Oh, my dearest friend,

oh, my dearest brother,

oh, my dearest and best old army buddy.

Please don't take this the wrong way, but I need you to leave. For I am not my past, and that's all we share now.

I am not the man you once knew,

for I desperately needed to find a future far from all our aforementioned conquests. I fought hard to get here,

and this is a much safer place for me to stay.

CONSTANTS OF MY LIFE

Constant struggle, I envy you, for struggle is your creed and life blossoms from your essence. Constant endurance, you withstand long after others have given themselves over to self-pity. Constant focus, sharp is your gaze and steady is your aim through the distractions of life. Constant courage, you envelop fear, whereas others are choked by its heavy hands.

Constant mourning, are we not in union with each other, passing through the needle's eye from a love taken too soon? Constant pleasure, electric is your touch and cool is your kiss on a lover's soft, rose-petal lips. Constant rejection, deadly is your sting on the artery of an exposed and vulnerable heart. Constant pain, agonizing is your affliction as you rip through people's lives and extinguish any goodness found there. Constant joy, paradise is revealed in your eyes, and sadness is unable to find me in your arms.

Constant struggle, O constant struggle, I envy you most, for you give birth to the world around me and you make us all somehow better with your labors.

IN THE NAME OF

We've killed in the name of this,
we've buried others in the name of that. We've suffered for the profit of just a few.
We've falsely rejoiced in someone else's advancement over our own. We've clung to our grief as if it were a virtue. We've pushed the seemingly endless pain away, to deal with another day. We've kissed strangers and felt the emptiness of an intimate act absent of any meaning. We've lived afraid to die, while in discontent with all life around us. We've passed old friends, looking the other way because we wouldn't even know where to begin. We've pondered whether the one who broke our heart even had a heart of their own.
We've tried it all in the name of love. We've shouted horrible things to God above. We've never been so close to giving up.
We've had mornings where we've searched for a reason to even rise up. We've come to the end of our ropes, nothing left but to fall. We've fallen, and in our inward falling, we have found the answers. We've found our inner light, which brightens even the darkest of nights.

Upon my completion of inpatient treatment, my teammates from 7323 came to the hospital to pick me up. I can't tell you how much that meant to me, guys. "Todos pagan!"
The first thing I noticed after leaving the hospital was how quickly we live our lives. In the hospital, every minute of my day was spent in some sort of personal or group therapy, absent normal everyday

distractions like a cell phone, which is normally tethered to me at all times. Now, looking back on the experience, I can honestly tell you that I was much more nervous about leaving the hospital than I ever was going in.

Just not being a slave to the phone, to email, or to an ever-changing calendar of events every hour of the day was a huge weight lifted off my shoulders. The moment I stepped outside, I was instantly thrown back into modern-day life and all its trappings. I had become aware of how we are killing ourselves by having this instant access to one another. How fake everything is in comparison to the countless real conversations I was having with my fellow patients, physicians, and other mental health professionals. This shined a huge spotlight on the utter emptiness of social media relationships and personae. About a month after giving up alcohol, I attempted to write something to describe my world prior to going into the hospital versus after receiving treatment.

SLAVE TO PROGRESS

Emails, distros, junk mail, bills, person-to-person chats, group chats, phone calls, conference calls, texting, group texting.

Shit rolling downhill. Meetings upon meetings, and sometimes meetings about past or future meetings!

Gatherings, family, friends, work, neighbors, responsibilities, schools, airports, combat deployments, joint training deployments, vacations, personal counseling, marriage counseling, work flips, store trips, traffic jams, honey-do lists, honey-don't lists, cooking, cleaning, midnight terrors, aches, pains, hospital stays, surgery days, weddings, funerals, and maybe even a hobby or two.

Shit compounding, formations stacking upon formations. No one can really be who they appear to be because I'm *not* really who I appear to be. I'm not this positive, happy, funny, motivated person I pretend to be when in one of these controlled situations, alone with myself. I'm miserable. I'm lost. I'm scared!

Phone calls, instant messages, calendars, spreadsheets, PowerPoint presentations, reports, air requests, ammo requests, risk assessments, receipts, DTS credit cards, personal credit cards, and planning (plans for wealth, health, savings, and retirement) are necessary. Oh, and insurance policies. And if I'm lucky, I get to have the occasional thrill outside the online office that is tethered to my hand, but at what cost?

The ball of shit has become a fucking mudslide, moving faster and faster, becoming more ridiculous, and becoming more diluted, to the point that we're all drowning in a world of shit!

The endless news—local news, political news, party news, news about other news, sports news, and weather news. The cable TV, the streaming apps, the stocks, the movies, the movie stars, the nations, the wars, my debts, the national debt, viruses, vaccines, poverty, racism, reverse racism, ancestry, history, space, the universe, religious beliefs, religious griefs, crime, time, eternity, good, evil, heaven, hell, pics, chicks, dicks, chicks with dicks, lions, tigers, and the fucking social media bears, oh my!

Question   Where, if anywhere, am I in any of these separate things?

Answer   Feeding your runaway mind, numbing your hurting body, and starving your lonely heart.

Question   What if I'm mentally about to snap?

Answer   Snap (inwardly).

Question   What if I'm physically exhausted to the point collapsing?

Answer   Collapse (inwardly).

Question   What if I don't know who I am?

Answer   Spend some time observing your outer self (idea) from the viewpoint of your inner self (truth).

Question   What if right now I'm so heartbroken that I'd welcome death to take me from this agonizing existence? *Where am I then?*

Answer   Closer than you've ever been to rediscovering
              who you really are and restoring the necessary
              balance to your runaway world of chaos. Your
              own world exists only inside your own head. You
              are the only one who can heal your afflictions.
              Soon you will find a connection again with your-
              self, a playful connection, and you will experience
              the joy that springs forth from within yourself,
              the source of all existence.

Closing diagnosis: You're a victim of your own success, you're a slave to
your own progression, and you're carrying too much of the past and the
future around with you in any single present moment. This is where
you stop. This is where you rest. This is where you ask for help. This is
where your outward journey ends and your inward journey begins.

IS THERE?

Is there anybody out there? Is there anybody who cares? Is there anything above
me? Is there anything deep inside me? I see my shadow just below me. I wonder if my shadow even knows me. Is there anything in my life?

All I feel is my pain and strife.

Can anybody hear me?

Hell, can anybody just beer me? Is there anybody out there?

Is there anybody who cares? I made a promise to myself to one day go and get some much-needed help. However, I never found the right time to talk about things weighing heavy on my mind. That day still hasn't come my way.

That day still feels very far away.

Maybe I did wait until it was too late.

Maybe it is just my unfortunate fate. Please, heaven, open up your gates. Is it ever really too late?

Can anybody really see me? Can anybody really free me? Here I am, on my knees, with tears running down both my cheeks, just looking for a little grace.

I ask someone up above me to have mercy and hear me.

I need someone who really loves me. I need someone who can really hold me. Raindrops start falling down all around me. I hear their gentle pattering on the leaves as water splashes down from the trees. Heavy rain makes for such a beautiful sound. While puddles are forming here on the ground, the wind whispers in my ear, "Don't you shed any more tears.

"All the beers in the world couldn't change your pain. Yes, there's someone who's really out here. Yes, there's someone who really does care. Yes, there's someone up above you. Yes, there's someone who truly loves you. There's a light there deep inside you. Today your pain is washed away from you. It's time again to go play like a child. Laugh out loud with a big old smile. You've always had in me a best friend. This is far from your story's end. "You were never really alone. You've always had a place to call home. With your arms stretched high and reaching upward, you feel the presence of I-love-you."

Now I laugh with tears of joy like my parents did when the doctor said it was a baby boy. All the pain stains wash away in due time. With all the hurt and all the grime, I'm telling you, my friend, I have a whole new life. I love my life, and I love my wife!

I'm reborn, unscorned. Hello, new day. Just come on out with me and play. Some of the best things happen on rainy days. With outreached hands reaching high up above you, yes, sir, there's someone who really loves you!

THE HIGHWAYMAN

(1) Man is born.

(2) Man grows into his body.

(3) Man, all of a sudden, requires a car to move himself through the world around him.

(4) Man upgrades his car as he goes, feeling more accomplished the newer and more expensive his car appears to the outside world. (5) Man gets on the interstate and only uses the off-ramps with gas stations visible right near the exits. Man refuses to use the exit ramps that are absent of any signs advertising gas stations ahead. (6) Man never gets anywhere. He only ever keeps fighting the hustle of traffic, stopping briefly only to fill up along the interstate, wondering where these other exits could possibly lead to.

(7) Man, one evening, out of pure frustration with a traffic jam, takes the next exit ramp, which has no sign advertising a gas station ahead. (8) Man discovers not only that there is no gas station, but also that this exit is absent an immediate on-ramp. There's only a one-way road parallel to the interstate leading in his original direction of travel. (9) Man goes for miles and miles, observing the interstate but unable able to get back to it. A little later, he is forced to turn right, now moving away from the interstate that he so desperately wants to get back onto. (10) Man drives car until it inevitably runs out of gas.

(11) Man, in denial, waits in his car that's out of gas, convinced some-one will eventually find him.

(12) After a day or two, man grows hungry and thirsty.

(13) Man reluctantly abandons his comfortable car and begins walking in a search for gas.

(14) Man goes and goes until his feet hurt so bad that they can't take him any farther.

(15) Man, all of a sudden, notices a rickety old bus stop with a bench right as he has loses the desire to continue. (16) Man sits down in an effort to rest his feet, reluctantly allowing himself to wish for a bus to come, but one never does.

(17) Man painfully begins walking again. (18) Man finds himself a few more miles down the road, again in the same beaten-down shape he was in earlier, and when taking his final step, he notices yet another random old rickety bus stop bench. (19) Man sits down, again wishing for a bus to come, but no bus finds him there.

(20) Man begins to curse loudly. He screams at the heavens to curse all the stupid people who initially put bus stop benches in places where buses have possibly never run. (21) Man reluctantly begins walking again, driven by his hunger and, now, his unrelenting thirst for water.

(22) Every step is excruciating. Man falls to the ground amid a plume of dry dirt.

(23) Man can't take another step, and this time, there is no bus stop bench to sit and rest his blistered feet, so man, having no other choice, begins to crawl in agony. (24) When man is so beaten down and exhausted that he can't crawl another inch, at that exact same moment, he bumps his head on another random old rickety bus stop bench. (25) This time, man rolls over on his back in the dirt and begins to pray.

(26) Man says, "I can't do this anymore. I need help. If you are out there, God, please help me. I need you now. I can't do this on my own anymore. Please save me, God."

(27) Man collects himself, gets up, sits on the rickety bench, and begins to wait.

(28) It starts to rain, and man gets soaked, but he also receives the gift of water, which quenches his thirst and washes him clean of most of the dirt that had caked his skin. (29) After the rain passes, the sun comes out from between the clouds, and with it, the wind begins to blow, and man becomes dry again. (30) Man, feeling better, starts to look around and enjoy all the sights and sounds of the forest that once was the bars to his cage. (31) Man sees beauty in the lit parts of the forest where there had once been only imagined fearsome things in the dark. (32) Out of nowhere, a bus pulls up, moving in the direction man has been traveling, away from the highway. Its doors open. (33) Man gets on the bus with absolutely no destination in mind, just grateful for the bus and its driver. (34) Man finds other people already on the bus, some of whom are sitting blissfully and looking out the windows, and others of whom appear to be peacefully sleeping, almost motionless. (35) Man sits down and asks a woman next to him, "Where are we going?"

(36) Woman replies, "No one knows. Each of us has our own destination ahead of us, but the important thing is that we don't pretend to know at this point in our journeys. However, we have great faith that we will *feel* our destination when we see it. We are all tired, broken travelers like you, and we all now have a growing faith in the bus driver, who knows the path before us that will eventually lead us to where we belong. So, we sit back to observe the journey, enjoying the ride, and we trust the bus driver knows the way forward."

(37) Man looks blissfully out his window, acknowledging that he doesn't know the future or his destination—and that's OK because the bus can get him there; the bus driver knows the way forward. Additionally, he has a newfound faith in himself, confident that he will know his destination when he crosses paths with it.

BOUND ONLY BY TIME

Bound in time, I am wrapped up in my mind. I am but a bird in a cage, a cage that allows me to see a world outside, but a cage that confines me all the same. Enraged at my cage, I am now aware.

Now that I can see,

now that I can feel its hold over me,

I throw myself at it in distempered rage, fighting to get out, fluttering to fly free, a beautiful freedom just beyond my reach. I hurt myself again and again with each failed attempt to escape. Calm is needed to gather my wits. Rest is needed to gather my strength. Time is needed to study my cage. People passing by me do not notice me, so I begin to sing to them.

I begin to engage with my cage's creators. One by one, they begin to notice me—notice me by my pleasant-natured chirping. One by one, they begin to touch my cage. Now, in their effort to interact with me, it happens: A person shows me the door to my cage. Over time, another, then another, then another shows me the series of movements needed to open the lock. One morning, just before the sunrise, I set myself free. I've never felt so free!

I've never felt more like me!

Truly there are no limits to this. *Bang!*

Some unseeable force now keeps me from the world, which is now so close. This is a bigger cage outside my smaller cage. I return to my small cage and lock the door before anyone knows I've mastered the lock.

With a little time, I will find the next door. With a little singing, I will be of a pleasant nature. With a little hope, I will one day touch those blue skies. With a little faith, I will return to set others like me free. This morning, I took notice of a bell noise—a bell noise always in the background of my day-to-day life. But this time, I looked and took notice of its origin. Wouldn't you know it, it's above what appears to be another door. I'm truly bound only by time.

HENCEFORTH INTO THINE OWN DESTINY

Henceforth, let there be only light.

From this day hence, into each passing night,

bring not the chains of weary sorrow with thyself into tomorrow. Upon all spots of darkness, shine forth with radiant power, from the truth of thine own enlightened spirit. For there is no going back into dim shadows, unless it be by thine own treacherously retreating authority. Thou art free to flourish and prosper with thine own knowledge shining forth from within endless depths. Give not counsel to thine own ignorant past.

Set not limits upon thine own untold future.

Root not in any moment that hast already proceeded, nor save thine own waters for any harvest yet to be. Give now thy water to thine own seeds at thine own feet. Harvest each moment with humility and grace in front of naysayers and passersby. Harvest each moment with no expectation for any measure of thine own rich fruits fully mature. For thee now knoweth the truth: Thou art the sun, the earth, the wind, and the rain of thine own spirit of destiny.

PART VIII

THE HIGHER SELF

"The ability to observe without evaluating
is the highest form of intelligence."
—Jiddu Krishnamurti

MOMENT IN TIME

From forever came time; from time came a moment.
There was no beginning before the end and no end before the beginning. Neutral is the faceless Creator from whom all life comes.

This Creator shows nothing without showing everything, be it in the heavens as we slip deeper into starlight's past or in that past, where see a moment into our future.

Or be it in breath as we fill our lungs for the last time.
In that moment, we find peace in life's final exhalation. Or be it in balance as our soul's time begins with the opening of our eyes for the first time. Feeling the warmth of light's kiss, another soul shares this moment as its eyes close for the last time, experiencing the feeling of darkness's cool as it envelops.

We exist in the spaces between the fabric of an eternal blanket, the timelines of thread woven throughout the moments of our lives. Never was your time's end more certain than in the moment of your beginning. Now what be the point? We cry out as the sands of life pour through the hourglass of time faster and faster. The point is this: Love—love—is the only force that breaks the power of time. Love suspends time in a moment, and a single moment can last forever without end. Love is our greatest moment and is how we find purpose in the foreverness of time. Therefore, live,

Knowing you will die and find love along the way.

In that moment, however brief, live forever free.
From forever came time, and from time came a moment.

AZTEC GOLD

I close my eyes and punch through to the other side.

Everything's connected. Everything is flowing, expanding, and yet somehow collapsing.
There's no right and no wrong, no good and no bad,

Just existence, just being. All is life source. All is reverberating and manifesting in an endless process of creation. Like sacred geometry playing within its own awareness, kaleidoscope patterns pulsate like Aztec gold as I go deeper and deeper into myself.

Why am I here?

Because I simply chose to be.

My life force, my essence, expresses itself in a physical form, but I am not this body, and I am not this mind. Yes, I have collected a body, and yes, I have collected a mind, but I am not these things.

After I leave this body, it will be of no further importance. It will return its borrowed stardust to our Mother's crust.

We are all connected. We are all conscious expressions of the collective. There is a steady humming behind everything. It can be heard as well as felt. As the air fills my lungs, I remember where I have anchored my body. Soon I will be back in my mental projection, and soon I will return to my physical form, but I am not my vessel, and I have no form.

I belong here, connected to the source, but in order to grow, I chose to experience a physical form.

Slow breathing leads to peace and serenity as the air splashes against my skin. Grateful I am for the warm blood I feel pumping through my veins as I take my form once more.

I am alive and I am here because I still choose to be. Here, where there is life.
Here, where there is death.
Here, where there is space and time, but these things exist not outside this place.
There is just pleasant awareness, and I remember now why I came.

I came by my own choice, simply to exist.

My only desire is to expand, and in my efforts to expand, I breathe deeply into myself.

WHAT IT'S LIKE

What it's like is as close as you can get to it.

If you attempt to hold it, it becomes formless.

If you attempt to see it, it becomes unseeable.

If you attempt to express it, it becomes inexplicable. If you try to speak it, it slips between the letters of the words unsaid. If you attempt to corner it, it hides behind you. It's outside the whole and inside the nothing. It's in a relationship with itself, and it equals zero—the sum of the collective. It's here, it's there, and it's everywhere in between. If you attempt to think it, you only think yourself. If you try to feel it, you only feel yourself.

If you think you have somehow smelled or tasted it,
then you've done neither. But if you can let go of the pursuit
of it, it will be so. What it's like is as close as you can get to it.

SUN NEVER SETS

There is always light from day to night. The sun, our father, doth not set; he uncovers each subject undyingly anew. The moon, our mother, graces us as she paces behind him in glowing reflection. We waltz with their child as a playful partner upon the solar stage's ballroom floor. Can you hear the music? Can you feel the tempo?

Round and round we go, all together and all aboard.
Disrobe yourself, please—I beg of you.

> There is no death to the created,
> only death to an idea.

Nothing could be more untrue than the idea that we are the ruminations of our parents. We are each brought into view. The sun never sets, and neither do you.

RAINDROPS FALLING

There
has never
been, and there will
never be, a molecule
of H_2O that hasn't
been a raindrop,
an ocean,
a river,

a
cloud,
a flake of
snow, or an
iceberg,

each
a unit of
the collective,
forever moving
through unseen
forces from
divine bodies:
our sun, our
galaxy, our
universe.

Not
one
molecule is
different. Not
exempt.

Not
exempt
from, outside,
excluded from, or
the center point of this
harmonious process. This
eternal balance, this cycle
of endless change within
varying degrees of
consciousness,

states
of vibration,
states of frequency,
states of rhythm,
states of formation,
collects to form the
raindrop's body.
We exist

in free fall,
between the
higher,

lighter
planes

and
the lower,
heavier planes,
each unit existing
forever, all the same
within the all.
Therefore,
please fear not
your death
because
nothing

ever really
dies.

You
are once
again becoming
the endless ocean,
the collective seas,
the winding rivers,
the soft white snow,
bringing forth
with you

the
essential
conditions
for life—life
expressing only
itself,

life
reflecting
only
itself,

life
nursing
only
itself,

moving,
transitioning
repeating
as the sun
again helps
you

shed,
strip,
purify,
and transform,
releasing you
from any heavier
elements,

thereby
allowing
you to reascend
into the heavens,
physically
manifest,

and
begin a
new cycle
of harmonious
manifestation.
We are

but
raindrops
falling. May the
winds be
kind to
you and guide
you on your
journey.

DISTANT DREAMS

Distant dreams have long since passed
like reflective stones through sharp stained glass. Thoughts fade
as the body dissolves. Conscious waves against timeless resolve
drift softly through cracks in sand, through shapes abnormal
on sounds of land. Dripping dreams shout songs in time,

splashing paint across the canvas mind. Spinning bubbles create a dizzying dance within the lungs. The breath strokes the rhythm with its drum. Laughing children play while jumping rope. Screamed sorrows are heard from a drowning boat. Dimmed expressions of great depressions, words take form within a dream's progression. Raindrops fall into splashing puddles. Flowers root within the pillowed pools, passing away with the dying light.

Dark-lit troubles within Satan's bite, against comforting smiles of angels with their grace. Waves return upon your shoreline's face. A peaceful awareness soon reminds you of a life once lived with vibrant vines lying in silence between offset worlds. Unfurled eyes catch wind and pop open, awake. The dream seems long since to have passed, though it is only moments old. Distance within time is no measure of this dream's story told.

RISE ANEW

Avert your eyes from the sunset's dying light. In your heart,
feel the sunrise anew.

Refrain at day's end with song and conviction. Let loose your trumpets
as they roar in disobedient action. Death should stand in waiting.

Frustrated by the postponement of your vessel's launch
from the riverbank.
Frenzied with spiteful conviction amid death's request to willfully
extinguish your flame.
Burn to the last with no cause for apologies.

Inspire your actions to echo across heaven's halls, raging from a life well
lived.

With the power of your being, fan the flames of sunset's dying light.

In your heart feel the sunrise anew.

COLLECTIVE SUM

I'm the collective sum,

A universe within this one, without any
Deep oceans found in my eyes,
Depths still unexplored.

I'm drawn into this abyss
As the light from above fades away.
A river springs forth from the deepest trenches,
Flowing in a current of endless emotion.
A faint glowing from below begins to glimmer.
The mantle of my mind is burning.
Folded pressurized desires birth red-hot amber fires
On this cradled surface of conscious creation.
With my passions collecting, clashing, and spewing forth,
I follow deep, vast caverns down, down, down.
Not a single thought can be found, found, found.
Several layers deep, below my crust,
There is no core, but a door instead. I fall through the keyhole in the
floor and
Reemerge into the endless stars. From afar, I drift, afloat in the divine ether.

Stars are swirling around me in rebirth,
A galactic nervous system that feels
A collective connection to all sensations.
Nothing's unplugged from this network.
Everything within creation can be felt.
An idea begins to form, then it storms to be born,
Bringing with it the creative thunder of God.
A bolt of lightning flashes with a great, clamorous bang!

Outwardly expanding violently into awareness,
Inwardly collecting, intelligently selecting,
Fragmenting into spiritual bodies,

Wreathing into places and spaces within time,
Coalescing around the light of the original spark,
Planets of ideas make beautiful waltzing partners.
Galaxies spin within the collective.
Here, I now see, I brought nothing with me,

Nor did I leave anything behind.
Manifestation causes intense amnesia.
Who am I? Where was I? How did I come to be here?
I am a spiritual hangover from a mortal birth,
Desperately laboring, searching the collective sum of life,
Attempting to find something,
A feeling of lost truth somewhere out there.
Long looking without eyes to see,
Turning over every rock,
Looking under every bottle,
Asking anybody if they've seen me before,

Wondering if anybody could tell me who I really am.
Along my way, I begin to see reflections of the self
Stretched out within the faces of those I pass,
Somewhere scattered among the twinkles in each of their eyes.
One day, desperately tired from searching,
Absent of any recognizable truth,
I collapsed to get some much-needed rest.
Then I fell back into sanity,
Reflecting without cause,
Open without expectations.

A gentle voice in my heart spoke distinctly,
Seeding an idea.
That idea formed and imploded,
Imploded into expansiveness.
In a flash of light, truth banged forth.
I am the collective sum of the totality of all,
Outside of nothing, flowing back into everything,
The collective sum from a single source within the light.
I am something from the nothing,
Manifesting on all plains simultaneously,
Pulling the sum total of my ideas into this reality.
Therefore, I believe life is the collection of all our creative powers.

PART IX

THE CREATIVE CHILDLIKE SELF

OK, here I would just like to point out that throughout this whole process of self-discovery through writing, I admit that after a while, I started to feel much better. Weird, right? In the beginning, there was just a lot of fear, uncertainty, anger, and/or aggression coming through myself onto the pages. But after getting it out in a constructive manner, which allowed me to revisit issues if I was triggered by something, I found that I still enjoyed writing. I even noticed that some of my writings were more playful, uplifting, and confidently pushing the boundaries of what I thought I may be able to express as a new writer/poet. Honestly, I almost didn't include these last few writings, but I wanted to show you that if you get all the dark, emotional boxes out of your subconscious basements, you can then begin to find new life in a world of endless creativity through other not-so-heavy experiences within your past. Some of these are just me finding ways to pass the time, and others are me trying to poetically tell you about a funny event in my past life. The point is that I am finally free to explore other parts of myself . . . which sounds sexual now that I am reading this final edit aloud. HA! But I digress again.

HONEYBEE, HONEY

I'm buzzing, searching for you, honey.
I'm here, honey.
My heart, it burns for you, honey.
I'm knocking on your petals, honey.
Let me roll around inside you, honey.
Let me come and play inside you, honey.
Your petals are open wide, honey.
We set each other alive, honey.
Timeless is our love, honey.
I feel not an hour inside your flower, honey.
Let me take you away from here, honey.
Let me fly you across the fields, honey.
Just slip into my hair, honey,
as we take off across the air, honey.
Yes, fly straight into the sun, honey.
Our fun has just begun, honey.
Look at all the world around you, honey.
The world exists just for you, honey.
Let me take you to my tree, honey.
Let me be your honeybee, honey.
With the use of just my wax, honey,
with the strength from just my back, honey,
I'm building you this perfect comb, honey,
a place to call your home, honey,

where you'll never "bee" alone, honey.
This golden amber city is for you, honey.
My song, my sting, I give to you, honey.
My life was meant for you, honey.
As I die, I die for you, honey.
As I fall, I fall into you, honey.
Let me melt into your arms, honey.
And please softly hold my little head, honey.
Let me be a bee for you, honey,
adrift in an endless sea of you, honey.
I'm forever with you here, honey.
You've called me to your home, honey,
where we will never be alone, honey.
No, I will never be a bee without you, honey.
I'm always right here with you, honey.
Yes, I'm always right here for you, honey.

VELVET SOUL

This poem lusters as it clusters.
Words jump aboard music's rhythm.
My heart beats as words take shape.
Verse after verse leaps to life from the nothing.
Passion pushes through my pumping blood.

Poetry rises up from my velvet soul. As I write these words on top of a beach of sand within my mind, lovers laugh as dogs give chase to the receding waters. Waves crash as my pen splashes against these pages. Yes, it's time to set these words free into the world. A kissing booth has become my mind.

Now sit right here with me in subtle silence, cutting yourself free
from any violence,

And rest your weary traveling bones next to mine as windy fingers slowly pass through your flowing hair. Patiently waiting, the world outside will still be there for us. We'll enter it again in due time.

BLUE WATER PASTURES

With prepped sheets, ready sails, and a rising tide both in the ocean and deep in his heart, the sailor casts his bowlines off and points his lady out toward the channel, moving into deeper watery pastures. All he can hear is the diesel engine's thumping as blue water diamonds dance across her hull. The promise of a new adventure whispers in the wind as the sun begins to crest over a beautifully lit napalm-colored skyline. The weather vane points the way as the craft's restrained boom squeaks back and forth, attached to her towering mast. His fingers feel an urging vibration in the wheel, a longing for him to let loose her restless legs. She longs to be pointed into iron, and thus, he leads her into the stables of a blowing breeze. He winches her lines as she screams, her sails free to embrace a teasing wind, and tightly ties her off. As the thumping ceases, the only noise to be heard is the fluttering of her anticipation. With a firm stance, he softly leans into her and alters their bearings.

As the wind catches her, her wild spirit jolts to form,
and to life, like a wild unbroken mustang springing from
a holding stall. Great joy overfills the sailor as he feels his lady
of the sea passionately galloping across blue water pastures.

The salty wind blowing through her mainsail gently cascades down her mizzenmasted tail with flirtatious flapping. His precious lady of the sea is freed to let be known all the deepest passions locked within her treasured, salty, and still wild, untamed heart.

JUST ONE MORE DANCE

Dancing, swaying,
Two panting lovers
In the dark
On the floor
Underneath glowing lights.
Gripping, grinning.
Hot sex spinning.
Locking eyes.
Pressing thighs
As we step, pull, and push.
Sweat swirling.
Hair twirling
As music pounds our insides.
Lips biting.
Disco lighting.
The DJ plays our song.
Holding tightly,
A habit nightly,
With eyes locking,
People flocking,
The jealous mocking us,
Envious of how we move.

You're busting, bursting. I'm begging, thirsting
For you, the woman of my night.
Bending, bumping,
Our heart rates thumping, I chase you,
The woman of my dreams.

But the night soon passes.
Lying there praying,
Still swaying,
Alone in my bed,
Thinking of the night just past. I need you, want you,
Have to ask you
For just one more dance.

RUBY-RED MUD

As I stood there on top of the white sands, watching the waves crash against the shoreline, there you appeared. You were set against an endless sea that was rough and beautiful, same as thee.

And the damn gulls cried out amid the sunset's glow as I felt the flow of soft sand pebbles, white as snow, running between my barefoot toes. Your hair was curling with the wind and salt swirling, oceans bursting, nay, thirsting to drink from another one of your salty beach kills. A million diamonds danced across orange-sparkled waters. Birds circled through the salty air, pleading for you to again feed them fresh meat, red, rare. With gulls giving mocking calls, and as sunset's light steady was falling, I began to look upon your body, gazing in admiration. I had never seen a figure more defined, so moline. You are a true predator by design.

Winds gusted against my back, and that was just enough to attract you, a pretty little shark, to commence your attack.

My scent, from a small drop of blood or a blood spot from a close shave just that morning, must have floated across the air and through your luscious hair. And those damn gulls cried out while the ocean roared. Paralyzed by your beauty, I adored

Your malevolent body as it moved and grooved, as if swimming on top of the sand. I remember the beach had the softest sands, just like your hands. With a tilted chin, you gave a grin, the razor smile of a crocodile, but you were no crocodile; you were something with many more teeth. You turned and swayed, and gently preyed, as you circled me in your python grip, your serpent tongue hissing a sexy, seductive lullaby into my ear. Your beautiful ocean eyes had these strong pulling tides, and they pulled me right under as if a cannonball had been chained to my ankle and you used it to drag me down into your locker. Hungry, anxious gulls kept calling as the sunset's light steadily fell. You had me firmly in your grip. For me, it was much too late, and thus, you frenzied upon my flesh, biting me, thrashing me into little tiny bits.

You then slapped me and choked me with your little red piranha-like lips.

I pulled back on your hair as you began to scream, my eyes locking onto your deep, dead eyes under what had become dusk's dark blue skies. As you continued your feeding frenzy, we both began to sink deeper and deeper into the hot, wet sand below our bodies.

Those damn gulls kept crying out against sunset's final glow as my blood steadily flowed, staining the white- pebbled snow. The blood in your smile told me you had feasted very well. Truth be told, I liked it. It was blissful hell. Your viscous savagery was matched only by your majestic figure. My skin had turned red rare as you left me there naked and bare. I was just your catch of the day. Filleted prey, there I lay. My eyes had been ravaged by your forceful thighs. I truly was a salty, hot mess amid the crashing white tide.

My ravaged eyes last gazed upon your face as you rose up off my limp body like a black widow that had just finished drinking her cocooned lover. With little morsels of my flesh still in between your razor teeth and with little chunks of my flesh still resting under your eagle-like talons, surely the taste of me was still upon your blood-soaked tongue as you sliver-swam away to go find your next prey. You had trophied pieces of me back out to the sea, where you will always be free to hunt. Those damn gulls with their unrelenting calls just kept at it. As the sun finally slipped below the horizon, I couldn't move, still paralyzed, so I just lay there applauding you, for you had devoured me. I now knew how it felt to be the prey of an apex predator. I had been the big fish in my small pond, but you had shown me the great, big ocean and how deadly beautiful it could be. The ocean's waves under the dark night skies continued to lap from my freshly severed veins. Moon's later light would have shown you my absolute delight as I lay there on top of what had become ruby-red mud, just smiling at the stars and wondering if I'd ever again find another shark like you.

POPPING GENIE TOPS

A vow I make with you, my mate, never to leave your side, but first you must give me your trust and take this little ride. A sprinkle of this, a sprinkle of that, as we pop a genie's top. You're so much fun, my only one, so please don't let this stop. Now, storms, they come, and storms they go; it's all a part of life. Death's a door, and time's its key, opening the other side. But until then, we give a grin, though rolling tears persist.

With songs and laughs, we will find our paths as they merge again, becoming one. So, laugh out loud at sad-faced clowns as our hearts both burn brightly with pleasant smiles on our faces. It's all for fun. Life's just begun; good times are on the tides.

A sprinkle of this, a sprinkle of that, and this poem has got to stop. But the next time we're here, let's grab a beer and pop another of these genie's tops.

WORDS ARE A MIGHTY SWORD

Words become a mighty sword of affirmation for those who master-fully wield them.

Stand with me for a moment here on top of this cover sheet. Look with me up and out, into the great unknown. It's beautiful in its endless creative substance, daunting in its task, and a little unnerving in its size and scope.

It would be much more intimidating to be here without a sword in my hand. My sword contains an endless army of words.

My words are ready to stand up against any detouring force that dares to stand in our way in these sacred papered valleys.

This paper is good ground. Let us begin.

Broadcasting into the great unknown, I order affirmations to scout forward in the field of my heart's desire.

On behalf of the future I desire to manifest, I order my light infantry to advance!

Soon they clash with the forces of fear, uncertainty, and indecision.

I send powerful affirmations to aid them soon after first contact is made. These affirmations charge forth with the speed and thunder of a light cavalry company to rescue our deteriorating flanks.

This front line's flanks were always destined to deteriorate when any pressure was applied because their ranks initially were filled with recruits who had good-sounding wishes and who set out without absolute conviction that the dream would be fulfilled.

I cast these initial words out early in the manifesting of the dream state as I dare to speak them aloud.
Here, they find themselves overwhelmed by the unrelenting fears that seed doubts within these pages before us.

These savage fears began to countermarch on my army of words at the very moment I dared to dream *You, This Is Me . . . Over?* into existence.
These fears bring doubts, and doubt causes hesitation.
A hesitating front line always begins to buckle after the first wave of adversity. But look, my powerfully affirmed light cavalry is arriving now! Ha-ha, just in time.

See, my reinforcements—that is, my affirmations—push through the doubts of the opposition like a candle's light cutting into the darkness of night.

Behold my sword Gladius, a feathered pen. Release the poet!

From the tip of this feather, I forge together the powerful vibrations from my heart's own tongue.
With feathers, I fly through papered skies, which rain ink down upon the seedling ideas, which are scattered by the winds with each turning page.

The book of my soul is bound in fine weathered leather, crafted from the very hide of the beast from which I ascended.

With the pointing of my sword, I advance my army of words in a tight formation with a number of columns across these open fields of papered ivory.

Obstacle after obstacle is breached until I stand on top of a mountain of conquered pages.

I plant my flag high above the front cover of first formation; I gaze outward and inward at all I have created.

Atop the manuscript of *You, This Is Me . . . Over?*, I sheath my sword, again staring upward and outward into the great unknown.

I rest my words on top of this glorious campaign, for they have served me well, but we know the war is far from over.
My army of words will not lay down their arms, knowing that absolute victory is within our reach and that absolute victory is the destiny we have together chosen.

Words become a mighty sword of affirmation to those who masterfully wield them.

You see, the pen is not mightier than the sword; the pen is the sword!

AFTERWORD

Well, there it is, ladies and gents! You have taken a journey through my inner self—the good, the bad, the ugly, the spiritual, and the absolutely demented! It was me poured out on paper. Did you relate?

Did you put *You, It's Me . . . Over?* down, only to find the courage to pick it back up and continue reading? Did you lose respect for me, or did you find a piece of yourself in my words?

You may be asking yourself, "So, what now?"

My honest answer is that I don't know. And it's OK that I don't know.

You see, the thing about admitting to yourself that you don't know the future is that you're speaking the first truth in a long line of truths to follow. For me, it was the first real breakthrough in my recovery, opening up the possibility for a future that was better than anything I could have dreamed of when I was sitting where you are possibly sitting right now. I heard a good friend say one time in group, "You can't fix the shit in your head with the shit in your head."

God's truth is that none of us knows the future, although there are a lot of people who want us to believe that they do know our future. The fact is that the only thing you can really know in this life is yourself. I, like you, have spent most of my life trying to convince people I was anybody other than myself because I didn't know who I really was deep down inside, and I was terrified to look!

I know we all have a past, and some of us are desperately attempting to put as much time and distance between us and our respective pasts as humanly possible. All our unprocessed traumas, including our childhood traumas, are still inside us, trying to be acknowledged. I told you, I ran to an outer war with a war already going on deep inside me. I was young and naive, and at that time, I had my physical strength to lean on, but when my body began to fail, it took with it my identity. Hope was ripped out of my life when my body couldn't keep up with my ego's identity. However, my life didn't start out that way. I had hope as a child that I was somehow going to change the world for the better, but when my hope for myself was taken from me, my hope for this world went away with it. Fortunately, the human experience is full of second, third, and so forth chances. There is good news still at the end of your fall no matter how far you fell to hit your bottom.

You are not any one thing, my friend. You are everything because you have the divine spark within you. Now, if I were to tell you that you are God, your ego would likely take that knowledge to a very dangerous place. But if I were to tell you that you have a piece of God inside you the same way I do and the same way every single person you pass on the streets does, what would you do with that knowledge? If we all had this knowledge, then maybe we would start to treat each other better. Maybe we would learn to be more patient with one another. Maybe we would learn to actually listen to one another in order to be understood ourselves.

I know the horrors that are in this world because I have found them inside myself. I know hate is very real because I found hate inside myself. I know love is very real because I have found love inside myself. I know forgiveness is possible because I have found a way to forgive myself. I know elements of racism, sexism, intolerance, and selfishness are real because I found some residue of these things inside me. However, I know that compassion, understanding, healing, hope, and faith are also very real because I have found them all in abundance within myself. I learned to give all these things inside me a seat at the table and a chance to be heard. My writings are their voices on paper.

We are not the things that happen to us, we are not the bricks we pick up in life, and we are not supposed to know everything when we are in this human form. We are all pieces of the divine, interacting with one another. We are here attempting to have a human experience in order to grow and spiritually transcend our mortal limitations.

The enemy that defeats you, me, and all of us is the enemy you, I, and all of us refuse to acknowledge. It is using all of us to perpetuate itself. *How can it be that simple?* you might think. The explanation is easy: These things continue to thrive in our world because eliminating them would force each of us to do the one thing that most people fear the most, which is to change, admit our faults to ourselves and others, admit our limitations, believe in a power greater than ourselves, and look inward. You can't run from yourself; you follow yourself wherever you go. And I heard someone say one time that the things we run from run us!

Find your voice, be yourself, and own your truth. No one can be you, so don't waste your time attempting to be anything other than your true self. The only question is: Do you like yourself after you really get to know yourself at a deeper level? I hope you do, and if you don't? Maybe you are just a dick! No, not really, but maybe you are at this moment in time. If you like yourself the way you are? Then someone else out there will appreciate you just the way you are because they are that way too, and they also like themselves for the exact same reasons. However, if you have changed for the worse and no longer like who you've become? There is still time, and with this new awareness, God's grace, and a little help from all those who still love you deeply, mighty forces will come to your aid. Oh! That last comment was something my dad wrote on a piece of paper after he started chemotherapy. He wrote, "Be bold, and mighty forces will come to your aid; don't believe in defeat, and I can do all things through Jesus Christ who strengthens me."—Dan Dooley

And what if we all start to backslide? You might be wondering. Well, if I do start to regress in my chemical dependencies issues, you will know it quick because I will check my butt back into outpatient groups and begin attending daily meeting until I'm again on firm time-proven footing.

So, show yourself some grace. Be honest with yourself. And when you're strong again, be open to paying it forward to others who are currently hiding from themselves and attempting to outrun the pain they have accumulated along their life journey.

I have spent the majority of my life without my dad, but I can tell you with certainty now that I've always had a Heavenly Father watching over me. You do too! Remember, my brothers and sisters, heaven and hell are not faraway places. Heaven and hell are both found right here inside each and every one of us. As above, so below. As within, so without.

God bless you all, good luck, and take life one day at a time. I believe in you. If my word means anything to you at this point, then believe me when I say that you are so much more powerful than you have been led to believe! Life's just a lot of people helping people. It's a beautiful thing, and so are you.

My name is Clinton Beaudel Dooley. This evening, I feel grateful and blessed, and yes, I have accomplished my goal!

Can anybody out else out there hear me?

ACKNOWLEDGMENTS

A special thank-you to my editor, Melanie Hill, who is a veteran of the Royal Australian Air Force, a poetry major, a full-time editor, and a loving mother and wife. She is also someone who understood the why behind *You, This Is Me . . . Over?* with little to no explanation needed from me. Mrs. Hill just got it, so I owe her a heartfelt thank-you for helping us get this far along in the process of bringing into this world a book that I believe we can all agree is a sort of project that has never before been attempted.

Mrs. Hill can be found at melaniehill.com.au, or you can email her at melaniehillediting@gmail.com.

Support Your Local

SFBMC

B.F.F.B.

EST. 2006